# A Spiritual Life

*SUNY series*
*in Modern Jewish Literature and Culture*

Sarah Blacher Cohen, Editor

# A Spiritual Life

## Exploring the Heart and Jewish Tradition

### Revised Edition

## Merle Feld

State University of New York Press

Cover photo courtesy of Robert St. Coeur/iStockphoto.com

Published by
State University of New York Press, Albany

For information, contact State University of New York Press, Albany, NY
www.sunypress.edu

Production by Diane Ganeles
Marketing by Fran Keneston

**Library of Congress Cataloging-in-Publication Data**

Feld, Merle
    A spiritual life : exploring the heart and Jewish tradition / Merle Feld.
— Rev. ed.
        p. cm. — (SUNY series in modern Jewish literature and culture)
    Includes bibliographical references and index.
    ISBN 978-0-7914-7187-6 (hardcover : alk. paper)
    ISBN 978-0-7914-7188-3 (pbk.: alk. paper)
    1. Feld, Merle.   2. Jewish women—United States—Biography.
3. Jewish women—Religious life—United States.   4. Feminism—Religious
aspects—Judaism.   5. Feminists—United States—Biography.   6. Spiritual
life—Judaism.   7. Jewish religious poetry, American.   I. Title.

E184.37F45   2007
305.48'8924073—dc22
[B]                                                    2006101107

10 9 8 7 6 5 4 3 2 1

*for Lisa and Uri—*

*Hold fast your dreams and ride them high*

# Contents

# Preface

When *A Spiritual Life* was first published in 1999, I began to travel across the country giving readings to promote the book and to develop an audience for it. From Portland, Maine to Palo Alto, California, I was moved beyond measure to see the effect on audiences and readers as I shared the stories and reflections of my life. I discovered that I loved reading aloud this poetry and prose, but I also came to feel how much I wanted to use these opportunities to help the women and men who showed up to further their own spiritual liveliness and introspection. I wanted to expand and shift the focus from me, the visiting poet, to them, the readers in the room, encouraging them to listen more carefully and caringly to themselves and to one another.

As I accepted invitations to visit communities and campuses, I began to create techniques and materials that would allow "the audience" to become truly engaged, active. Invited as writer, I showed up as educator, devising questions for discussion that would at first draw close attention to my poems and prose, but that would then move outward to suggest how audiences and readers might explore the deep meaning of their own lives, with my writing as a jumping off point rather than as an end point.

I found myself thrilled, fascinated, and humbled facilitating conversations among audiences about the themes of the book to see how I could develop materials that fostered trust and stirrings of deeper community through the humanizing, reflective sharing which the poems and prose of *A Spiritual Life* inspired. Particularly when invited to communities as scholar-in-residence, I relished the luxury of time to develop and facilitate programs for adult learners on study retreats, congregants in synagogues, college students in academic courses and in informal Hillel groups on campus. The book gave me a place to stand as I opened my spiritual life and my heart to be a source of teaching. And then after years of doing this teaching in person, I began to see the possibilities of coming full circle and allowing the book itself to serve as a resource through the addition of a chapter that could guide readers in my stead. Thus was born the idea for an educational tool to accompany and enrich this book, one that went far beyond the usual page or so appended by publishers intended for book groups.

First and foremost then, what is new to this revised edition of *A Spiritual Life* is the Readers' and Writers' Guide featured in chapter 12. Both the techniques and the discussion questions offered there have benefited immensely from my encounters and work with readers from across the country and indeed, around the world—in fact, the Guide would not exist at all without the ongoing response from readers—and so it is no wonder as I worked on this revised edition and most especially as I created the Guide that I felt myself accompanied by countless partners in spiritual journeying. I am filled with gratitude for the open hearts that welcomed the first edition of *A Spiritual Life* and for the energy, excitement and pleasure I have been privileged to give and to receive from so many readers and audiences. A special thank you as well to Gail Reimer and Rachel Jacobsohn whose thoughtful critiques of the Guide helped me to realize my vision.

Of all the encounters with readers and audiences, perhaps none had a greater effect than the experiences I was privileged to share with so many people in the former Soviet Union. (A fuller version of this remarkable story is found in chapter 8, "Repairing the World: The Work of Tikkun Olam," also a new chapter to this book.) In brief, I traveled to Belarus in 1998 with Project Kesher, a Chicago-based nonprofit that helps to foster emerging women's leadership and Jewish life in

the FSU; during that visit I made some of my poems available
to Jewish women's groups there and eventually there was a
compelling demand to translate *A Spiritual Life* into Russian.
With the help of dear friends Juliet Spitzer and Phil Wachs,
Esther and Max Ticktin, Ruth and Rob Goldston, and many
others in the Princeton community where I once made my
home and still feel so at home, *A Spiritual Life* was rendered
into Russian (as *"The Life of the Soul"*) and subsequently in 2003
I went on a three week book tour of Ukraine.

During those extraordinary weeks, described here in
chapter 8, I not only read and taught from the book, but in
the late night hours when we should have been relaxing and
sleeping, my companion and beloved fellow activist Nina
Klotsman, and my gifted translator Lyubov Zrazhevska, col-
laborated with me to create a curriculum for Project Kesher
Jewish women's groups across the FSU using *"The Life of the
Soul"* as its base and inspiration. How delighted I am that that
work there so enriched and informed the Readers' and Writ-
ers' Guide here in chapter 12. My experiences in the FSU
were a profound teaching for me and thus reinforce once
again the irony of "giving" and then discovering that your gift
has been returned to you one-hundred-fold: English-speaking
readers enjoying this revised edition will benefit immeasurably
from Russian-speaking sisters and brothers across the sea whose
insights inform much of the Readers' Guide.

Further cross-cultural influences on this revised edition
are the result of a request to translate *A Spiritual Life* into
Hebrew. That appeal came after the beginning of the second
*intifada,* and because I felt the original book, published in
1999, would seem woefully outdated to an Israeli audience, I
worked to give the Hebrew translator a more current chapter
on Israel (chapter 7, revised here) and used the opportunity
to further reflect on themes, experiences and issues relating to
Israel. I later remarked to friends as I prepared this revised
English edition that it is really "an English translation of the
Hebrew"—said jokingly, but in fact, an accurate appraisal. The
Hebrew version is not yet published: I feel great excitement

and curiosity to see how Israeli audiences will respond to this poetry and prose.

One last explanation of this revised edition is in order, namely, how did chapter 12 come to include not only a Readers' but also a Writers' Guide. Back in the mid 1990s, I had begun working with a variety of constituencies using writing as a means of helping them explore interior realms. By 2000, at the invitation of Rabbi Bill Lebeau, I was leading spiritual writing workshops for rabbis at the Jewish Theological Seminary's Rabbinic Training Institute; the workshops were quite effective and in the second year of my offering them, Bill asked if I would continue this work with rabbinical students at JTS. One thing led to another, dear old friends Joyce and Mike Rappeport were inspired to encourage me to expand my work to include students at Orthodox, Reconstructionist, Reform and nondenominational rabbinical schools, and with help from Joyce and Mike's Albin Family Foundation, the Rabbinic Writing Institute was born. Using techniques I've developed over time, I enable rabbinical students to connect to the core of their own spiritual lives and then to teach from that place of authenticity and wisdom, inspiring congregants, students, audiences, and readers to know their own deep core of meaning. It is to Joyce and Mike and Bill that I owe a debt for the most fulfilling and meaningful work of my life to date, and to my many beloved students who have enriched what wisdom I pass on to you in the Writers' Guide within these pages. The work I do guiding rabbinical students allows them to write about and to more deeply know and understand their own lives and stories, and it is my hope that this Writers' Guide will help you to do the same.

Thanks always to Director of SUNY Press, James Peltz, for his understanding and support of my work, and to Lisa and Eddie who never are too busy to read a draft of my writing and help to improve it with fine literary sense, keen intelligence, and love.

# Acknowledgments

There are a number of people who through their passionate appreciation of my poetry have encouraged me over the years not only to continue to write (that comes as it will, like the rain) but to save, collect, and transfer my words from scraps of paper to word processors; they have invited me to come read my work, have encouraged me to send it out for publication. Because they took my creative efforts seriously, they helped me to take those efforts seriously. My heartfelt thanks for their praise, which was offered early and often: Judith Plaskow, Ellen Umansky, Marcia Cohn Spiegel, Alicia Ostriker, Susan Reiman, Marcia Marker Feld, Roger Lewis, Ruth Schulman, Joyce Rappeport, Laura Spear, Leah Lemonick, Ruth Goldston, Amy Trachtenberg, Rev. Sue Anne Morrow, Kathy Murtaugh, Esther Ticktin, Joe Reimer, Henny Wenkart, Rabbi Deborah Brin, Rabbi Susan Schnur, Rabbi Patty Karlin-Neumann, Karen Kushner, Lorel Zar-Kessler, Michael Lerner, Ellen Frankel, Rabbi David Teutsch, Rabbi Reena Spicehandler, Rabbi Joe Levine, Rabbi Danny Leifer, Nancy and Louis Berlin, Alvin Mars, Janet Olshansky, Rabbi Michael Paley, Rabbi Devorah Jacobson, Rabbi Susan Harris, Rabbi Debra Orenstein, Rabbi Jane Litman, Rabbi Jim and Elana Ponet, Sharon Strassfeld, and Barbara Dobkin.

A singular acknowledgment to Jean-Claude van Itallie, my teacher in theatre: I remember an afternoon when we sat together in a rustic cottage at his retreat Shantigar and shyly, haltingly, I read him my first poems. In that hour he taught me everything I know about giving my words to an audience.

Three people especially are responsible through their stubborn devotion for not allowing me to finally be beaten down by the long and arduous effort to find a publisher for this volume. Fred Bernstein went so far as to inaugurate a career as literary agent on my behalf; Judith Plaskow offered her keen mind, her critical eye, her loving affirmation; from the very beginning, Gail Reimer gave unselfishly of her time, her energy, her considerable gift for reading a text, helping me envision the unique structure of this book. My deepest gratitude for the many years of friendship and love I've shared with each of you.

I count my blessings that Sarah Blacher Cohen (seemingly not content simply to bestow good fortune on me by publishing a play of mine) invited me to submit this manuscript to SUNY Press; that James Peltz read it in a night and fell in love with it; that he, Diane Ganeles, and Fran Keneston have taken me through my first experience in publishing with an astonishing display of kindness, professionalism, and solicitude. Warm thanks as well to Nancy Trichter who represented me in writing "the marriage contract" and to Lisa Feld who offered her companionship and skill as tonic for the usually dull chore of proofreading.

For acts of friendship and bottomless devotion through dark nights, there can be no adequate acknowledgment on these pages—only in the daily living of my life can I return the love and care I have received from Frima Fox Hofrichter, Debora Phillips, Aaron Lemonick, and Leighton McCutchen.

Finally, Eddie. Much of the above and more have I received from you. All these years and all these roads later, your soul is still the soul of Ein Gedi.

# 1

*Beginnings*

# A Spiritual Life

A few years ago a Jewish magazine decided to devote an issue to spirituality and asked me to contribute a short piece describing "a spiritual moment." I thought, a moment is best captured in a poem, I'll submit a poem. In fact, I submitted not one but two poems, two very different poems. The first captured a poignant memory of packing away my Passover dishes one year, an act which forced me to acknowledge that the holiday had come and now was gone, that my unspoken, unconscious longing to see my mother during a holiday so full of childhood memories, my mother who had been dead already several years, was of course a longing unrealized, unrealizable. In the poem were the tears of my feeling abandoned by her, abandoned in the Universe, alone, alone, so alone. Out of the depths I call to you . . .

The other poem, a very different moment, though actually also a moment of tears. A twenty-year-old me sitting down to Friday night dinner for the first time with my life's partner-to-be. He began to make kiddush, the traditional blessing over the wine, and I was overwhelmed by feelings of gratitude that my journey had delivered me to love, to shared meaning, to connection. As the Psalmist sings in Hallel, "The stone that was discarded is now the cornerstone." In the poem I felt like that once discarded stone, as I sang out with joy through those old tears.

The Jewish magazine decided they had room for only one poem. For a while I thought I'd insist "both or none" but finally I gave in and told them to use the one with my Passover dishes: it seemed an unusual moment to share with readers, at least it could make them reflect on the idea that "a spiritual moment" was not only a moment of consummation, that a spiritual moment might equally be a moment of longing, of stretching toward something precious that was out of reach.

But really, what I wanted to do in offering both those poems was to give a glimpse of the complexity of terrain which constitutes spiritual geography. In some sense, I've been waiting in these intervening years for an opportunity to share not one, not two, but many many pictures of the life of spirit. I've been waiting for an opportunity to share through stories, through poetry, the important life stuff I know something about—the struggle to become who you are, the work to achieve peace with your past, the search for meaning and the assertion of meaning. Increasingly when I'm asked to teach or speak, I am conscious of the constraints of the agreed upon topic, and I work to make room within it for what I think is really important to say, for what I think the audience, whether it knows it or not, is hungry to hear about. To break through the cerebral, the polite, the conventional, the pseudointellectual, and to speak face to face, human to human, heart to heart, soul to soul. Scary. Easier to write a well-reasoned paper with respected accepted sources and then just get up to the podium and read with expression. Much safer. But I never seem to be content with safe. I want alive. More and more I want alive.

As I write these particular words, wrestling with the creation of something new, something which has never existed before, I don't know how it's all going to fit together. It's a lot like the story of my life (it is in fact the story of my life) and women's stories are so complicated. (True of men's stories too? Probably, but for the moment I'm taking refuge in one of my particularities.) Women's stories: not a linear plot, but levels of reality simulcast on three or four different screens. How to tell one coherent story when you know you're not living one coherent story.

So, a patchwork. For a while I was a quilter and my favorite part of the whole process was gathering all the different pieces of fabric, seeing the explosion of color and pattern, and then creating a design which celebrated each individual piece but also maintained enough of a harmony for all the pieces to live together.

What are the pieces of this quilt? I lay them out on the dining room table: stories, poems, reflections, prayers. What happened to me as a child, what I've learned day to day as a parent, my experience of Jewish time and symbol and custom and text, the political and spiritual dimensions of living in a Holy Land, the longing to be loved and to give love, the pain and terror and challenge of living in community, the continuing evolution of my relationship to my parents both dead now for many years. These are the greens and blues and purples and yellows of my life of spirit.

Beginnings. You should always begin at the beginning. But where is the beginning?

Earliest of all I remember the sunlight. I am sitting on a child's chair, next to my grandmother. She had long white hair— actually, not "white," rather, yellowed, ivory. It was braided, then knotted in a bun. She's wearing a dark Old Country dress, it buttons down the front, covering a body which is sturdy yet soft. Black leather shoes lace up to her ankles, "old lady shoes." We are sitting in the sunlight, perhaps it is autumn. The warm sun penetrates me, embraces me, I feel relaxed, cradled. It is a sensuous moment, a moment of safety. Peaceful.

Now I am a little older. A busy street corner, a few blocks from home. We were holding hands, suddenly we are not. Separated from my mother, I look up: the older children, the adults, tower above me, they block my light, darken my piece of sky. No one is holding my hand. I am separate. Alone.

A memory that repeats itself, every year, year in, year out. It is Yom Kippur. My brothers and I are home from school,

5

everyone is dressed up in their best clothes. The adults fast, Roger and I compete to see who can "hold out" longest. Some of this is like everyday—competing in a game with my brother. But some is different—dressed up, sitting quietly in the living room. Most different of all is my mother: she sits in a chair reading to herself from a small elegant white leatherbound prayerbook, the edges of its pages embossed a shiny gold. It is her book, received at something called her confirmation. (We don't belong to a synagogue, can't afford Hebrew school for me, I never have a confirmation, never receive a small elegant prayerbook of my own.) She sits in the chair for a long time and what is extraordinary to me is that for 364 days of the year she busies herself responding to our needs, our demands, but on this day she says firmly, "Please don't disturb me." She is engrossed in her reading, her reflection; occasionally with her thumb and forefinger she rubs the bridge of her nose, signalling to me a headache, but clearly she is not much distracted by it. Many years later, living in Princeton, New Jersey, my street is blocked off each year for one day, a legal fiction which establishes private ownership by the university of this public thoroughfare. For 364 days of the year, my mother is our property—we push, we pull, she works, she cooks, she schleps, she listens, she smiles, she laughs, she touches as we beckon. On Yom Kippur, she closes off the street to traffic and quietly declares, "I belong to myself."

I am 16 years old, in high school. It is the end of my senior year. We go on buses from New York to Washington, D.C. for the senior class trip. We stay in a motel—a first for me. I am excited by the motel, by sleeping in a room with girlfriends (I've never done that before either). We drive around Washington at night, I am thrilled by the buildings and monuments lit up, my eyes are wide open. I don't come from New York really, I come from the province Brooklyn, I've hardly ever been out of it. The weekend is over, the bus brings us home in the dark, my classmates are singing—folk songs of the early '60s, Broadway show tunes. Finally I can sing no longer, I go to sit in the back of the bus and look out into the darkness. It hurts so much to be alive. Some of my favorite teachers have chaperoned this trip, a debate rages within me: could I trust my secrets to one of them, could one of them offer me relief, could one of them break through my isolation? I don't want to go home, I don't want to go home, the wheels of the bus go round and round, I don't want to go home, beautiful Washington with its white buildings lit up in the dark, beautiful Washington is getting further and further away, closer and closer is Brooklyn, the no exit apartment, the pain in the walls, in the linoleum of that apartment . . . One of my teachers sits down next to me, he senses the pain relentlessly throbbing, he senses that I am somehow in terrible trouble, he is caring, responsive, but he chooses the tactic of making me laugh—he doesn't have the courage to be a listener.

I am 18 years old, a camp counsellor in the Catskills. I am supposed to be taking care of a bunk of 13-year-old girls, but even though when fall comes I will be entering my junior year of college, this is my first time living away from home and these 13-year-olds know more about camp life and possibly life in general than I do. The troubles at home are unrelenting; deprived of the chance of a sleepaway college, I must be grateful for the free public education of the New York City system. I travel to Brooklyn College every morning by subway and return every night in time for supper. I jump at the chance to go away, anywhere, even to work at a low budget summer camp in the Catskills. But now that I'm here I'm thrown off balance, I'm afraid. I never realized the troubles at home that torment me are also so well known that in a strange way they are comfortable, safe. I don't know my place in this new world, none of the mirrors are familiar and so when I look from one to another to see who I am, I don't recognize myself. I am terrified, I feel myself coming apart. Each day I struggle to hold onto the reality of that day. One night I walk alone to the lakefront, I look up into the vast night sky, a canopy of stars. A prayer rises from the secret center of my soul: not, *please God, make my problems go away, solve my problems, make it all better, deliver me.* Not that, but, *God, give me the strength to live my life.* And I feel a response—I asked for strength, I have received strength. From the vast dark sky, a sense of peace descends, I am filled with a quiet sense of peace. Subtly, the balance has tipped—after this night I am no longer a child with adult feelings and voices and urges. After this night I am an adult, doing my best to reassure and shepherd the fearful child, to smooth her hair and hold her close, whispering, "It'll be alright. It'll be alright. Sssh . . . "

Many moments come after these moments, but these moments are the beginnings for me. The beginnings of spirit.

So many paths to spirit are available, how and why did my spiritual path come to be a Jewish one? A part of the answer to that question lies back in my senior year of high school. My friends from the honors classes are studying for the SAT's, going to visit magical places like Haverford and Wellesley, mailing in applications to Berkeley and Ann Arbor. These are the people I competed with on geometry tests, they were my lab partners in zoology, together we argued about the secret motivations of Iago. Then they packed their bags for Boston, leaving me behind. I asked my mother, aren't there scholarships for kids like me, isn't that who the scholarships are for? But she said no, scholarships don't cover everything. A few years ago, when Ruth Simmons became the first black woman president of Smith College, she movingly told the *New York Times* reporter how her impoverished siblings and teachers chipped in to supply her with clothes when she went off to college. But no one believed in me the way people believed in Ruth Simmons. That was the part that wounded, that was the part that damaged. Only 16, and already stamped "not special."

So there I was at Brooklyn College, riding the subway as I had in my high school years, taking a bag lunch as I had in my high school years, sitting in endless required survey courses, mostly not as challenging as the courses I'd taken in my high school years. And I accidentally showed up for a freshman reception at Hillel, the center for Jewish students on campus. After the formal program, I sat in the large auditorium, dutifully filling out a form I had been handed. Responding to the question of what committee I might be willing to join—it seemed impolite to express interest in nothing—I absently checked off "social action." My fate was sealed: the student chair of the committee wouldn't let me go. She had my address, my phone number, somehow with that check mark I had committed myself to a seemingly endless round of committee meetings to talk about and plan for "social action."

Now I regularly found myself in the Hillel building where almost everything was strange and new for me: some of the students wore *kipot* (head coverings for observant Jewish males), some would put on a record after lunch and do a few Israeli dances—imagine, in the middle of an ordinary day, between lunch and classes, the ecstasy of dancing. These fellow undergraduates would spend their free time arguing about a passage from the Bible, sometimes be so engrossed in a discussion of Elie Wiesel or Martin Buber that they'd cut class to finish it. Nothing remotely as interesting was going on in the student center. I stayed. I made friends, we met on Saturdays and went to synagogue together, I took classes in Job, in Jewish mysticism, I stopped eating cheeseburgers.

Everything was exotic, magical: eating in *sukkah* (a simple outdoor harvest booth especially constructed for the eight day autumn festival of Sukkoth), Friday night candles, black Hebrew letters on white parchment, praying—imagine, praying, at fixed times, using prayerbooks. Other people who were attentive to the world in the ways I had always been privately attentive to the world. Other people had a language, there was

9

a whole history of a language, to express the reality of spirit I had previously known only in my private world. I remained unique—it's not that I merged with the group, lost my individuality—but suddenly I wasn't so odd, wasn't "too serious." Suddenly I wasn't so alone.

I was intrigued by this thing called Shabbat: because God, after working to create the world, took a seventh day to rest, we as humans have the opportunity to rest, to be God-like. (I can't honestly say we are "commanded" to rest—it's not my language—I don't think I've ever felt "commanded" to observe Shabbat or anything else for that matter. "Invited" feels like a more accurate verb for me.)

My imagination was more excited by the notion of Shabbat than by anything I had ever encountered before and probably since as well. I had never previously seen the opportunity to transform my own reality so profoundly. Mostly I felt imprisoned by the limitations of my reality. Here was a way of reshaping reality, transcending reality, which called to me more alluringly than did the enticements of an LSD trip. By not turning on or off lights and so heightening my consciousness of the sun in its course, by putting aside my school assignments and telling the supervisor at my parttime job that I was no longer available on Saturdays, by going to services on Saturday morning and reading and discussing the biblical portion of the week, by preparing food ahead of time and inviting friends to come eat with me after services—once a week I was turning Saturday into Shabbat, making for myself a different kind of day, a new kind of reality. In a sense what I saw was the difference between my ordinary day-to-day Brooklyn life and my mother's once a year Yom Kippur. I too could seize the power to say, "I belong to myself" and I could do it frequently, regularly, once a week.

You could, if you wanted to enough, rearrange the reality of your life. You could make a life of heightened meaning, of deepened meaning. Our lives are filled with moments of spirit, extraordinary moments ripe with meaning and nourishment, if only we can remain aware. I increasingly saw the spiritual realm of my everyday existence as a vast uncharted territory which could be cultivated as I chose—I had control over the depth and potential of this everyday realm, to sanctify or not to sanctify: the food I ate, the sky overhead as it lightened and darkened, Shabbat, the study of text, the cycles of the year, community.

I understood keeping Shabbat and *kashrut* (traditional Jewish dietary laws) as the radical assertion of meaning, the creative imposition of Jewish meaning on my previously secular world: the epiphany was that I could have control over my spiritual life. This religious metamorphosis took place over the four years of college, during which time I lived at home. How did my parents and I navigate the potentially troubled waters of a "born-again" adolescent Jew in the bosom of a secular family? One case in point (some would say a quintessentially Jewish one) expressed itself through food.

When I was growing up we did not have a kosher home. My mother did not keep kosher, my grandmother did not keep kosher, in fact I had no idea if my great-grandmother kept kosher. We had ham in the house pretty regularly, we did not separate milk and meat. In college then, when I realized that I wanted to keep kosher, I was faced with a dilemma. I knew of peers in similar circumstances who kept a pot and pan for themselves, who ate on a separate placemat at a corner of the family table food they had prepared for themselves alone. I was horrified by what seemed to me such a divisive, holier than thou approach. I thought my mother especially deserved better from me. So I made my commitment to *kashrut* with a reversal of the common Jewish concession to America and its culinary delights—while the usual practice is to keep kosher at home and eat out *tref* (non-kosher food, forbidden in the Bible), I kept kosher when I ate out, but at home I ate the food my mother prepared for all of us. This unique compromise was my way of saying that when I am in control of my own food, I will eat as I see fit and express my intention to keep a kosher home when I am out in the world on my own. Meanwhile, I am living under my mother's roof, I will show her respect.

But the story doesn't end there. My mother, catching on to the growing importance of this way of life for me, stopped buying ham. She then began shopping at a kosher butcher. By my senior year of college she was using the everyday dishes for dairy and the fancy company set for meat . . .

In the tradition, there are three special commandments (*mitzvot*) for women: to light Sabbath candles, to separate a piece of the dough when baking challah, to go to *mikvah*, a ritual bath, after your monthly menstrual cycle. None of these "women's" *mitzvot* did I learn from my mother. What I did learn from my mother was to honor the path that each person takes, to honor the person and the path in all their uniqueness.

Just as I needed to accommodate my food requirements during these years, I needed to find a way to celebrate Shabbat in a home where Friday night was for TV and Saturday for cleaning and shopping. I spent most Friday nights and Saturdays with three friends who were also students at Brooklyn College, also from secular homes, also active in Hillel. This was my first experience with the pleasures of community. Friday night we'd walk together to the home of a newly married Orthodox couple. The small living room of their apartment felt warm, cozy. Gail, the young wife, served tea and cake. We'd sit, we'd laugh, we'd talk by the light of their Shabbos candles. Then the long walk home through the dark Brooklyn streets (observant Jews—which is what we were learning to be—do not drive or ride in public conveyances on Shabbat). Four friends, two young men, two young women, we never dated each other, but in those long walks home we enjoyed a special intimacy of friendship, conversations which ranged from the religious to the political to the psychological, conversations which had room for intellect and for gossip. The exhaustion at the end of a busy week, the lateness of the hour, aching limbs, and cold air on our cheeks somehow made the walk all the more delicious.

Saturday mornings we went *"shul* hopping" together—synagogue shopping. Within a mile radius of where we lived in Brooklyn were many different synagogues of many different persuasions and we tasted them all. Probably our favorite was a small down-on-its-luck Conservative congregation, populated mostly by middle aged and elderly men (when we walked in they would exclaim excitedly, "The young people are here!"). They were warm and unpretentious, the rabbi was interesting, his sermons often bridged traditional interpretations of the text and observations on the turbulent times we were living through in the late sixties. Then one of the four of us would invite the rest of our small band home for a lunch that inevitably seemed to feature tuna fish. We would argue some more about the biblical portion of the week, sometimes even lingering till the sun set and three stars in the sky declared the Sabbath was over.

The first rabbi I ever met was Norman Frimer, the director of Brooklyn College Hillel. He returned from sabbatical to find me amongst the crop of new active students and set about getting to know me. He himself was Orthodox, from a traditional family; his three sons all went to Orthodox day schools. But his understanding of the life of spirit transcended his own Jewish particularity. He never asked me whether I observed *kashrut,* whether I attended synagogue. He simply asked me to go for a walk with him. Quickly it was clear he had no interest in small talk. As God asks Adam in the Garden, Norman Frimer asked me: Where are you in the world? Unlike Adam, I was prepared to talk. And he listened. What power is the power of a true listener, bringing understanding, bringing healing, bringing peace. Over the years of listening, he helped me to ask the questions which were my questions. Occasionally he offered answers.

A few years after college, already married, I described to him the spiritual wilderness I felt myself wandering in. What can I believe in, how can I have faith, how do I know what direction is the right direction for me in this world? He answered me with, "It's time for you to have a baby." Long after, he shared his memory of that conversation: "You thought I was telling you that because you were a woman. You thought I was saying, motherhood is your proper role as a woman. And you were so angry you wouldn't look me in the eye, so angry to have your theological torments written such a prescription." Quite so, he knew me well, he had accurately read me. But he had been wise enough to hear the question I didn't know to ask then. In those years I didn't want children, was afraid of raising children, lacked the courage for children. He was telling me, the questions you are asking, questions of faith, of meaning, these aren't intellectual questions, they are the stuff of life, they can only be answered in the living of life, in the trenches. Your life has as much meaning as you invest it with. And that probably means focusing more time and effort on the lives around you than on the philosophical contemplation of self. And while there are many ways to engage in human intercourse, one of the most demanding and therefore potentially most rewarding, is through the growing of children. He knew what I was terrified of facing: that for me, the leap of faith was the decision to become a mother and there was nothing more I could learn poised, stuck, frozen, on the edge of that leap.

In the early stages of my Jewish exploration, my gender seemed irrelevant. I was faced with the enormity of gaining entry into an ancient tradition of which I knew nothing. So many "firsts"—going to synagogue, saying the blessings after a meal, celebrating the rich variety of holidays from the ecstatic dancing on Simchat Torah to staying up all night studying biblical texts on Shavuot. I vividly recall the first weekday morning service I ever attended, walking into the room and seeing men wearing *tefillin* (two small black leather boxes containing scriptural passages, bound by black leather strips, worn on the left hand and arm and on the head). I had never in my life seen *tefillin* and the sight of these men whom I knew engaged in their morning prayers was such an intimate scene for me that I felt embarrassed to have intruded with my presence—somehow I shouldn't be viewing what felt to me so private a moment. The furthest thing from my mind at that moment was to question why no one invited me to put on *tefillin.*

I wanted to understand the system, from the inside, on its own terms. If it had assigned a different place to me than to Yehuda and Norm, I wasn't disturbed by that. In fact, one year when the student board at Hillel was voting on whether or not to have a *meḥitza* at services (a curtain separating the men and the women during prayer, considered discriminatory by most contemporary feminists), I was one of those who voted yes. I thought, seeing the men was distracting to me while I was trying to concentrate on my prayers and I didn't want them to be able to see me either—I wanted my privacy. I was unconscious of not being counted in the *minyan,* the quorum for prayer traditionally consisting of ten Jewish males over the age of thirteen—there were always plenty of men present and I think I was unaware of a count and also therefore unaware of the fact that I wasn't being counted. Similarly, I didn't feel excluded or offended not to be called up to the Torah for an honor—I had no idea how to do all the intricate things they were doing up there—I was struggling to just learn the Hebrew letters and certainly felt in that context undeserving of an honor.

I think the first time my identity as a woman was a source of alienation or pain for me as a Jew was as an undergraduate in a Hillel class studying the third century rabbinic anthology *The Ethics of the Fathers.* I was reading along, blissfully engrossed in unlocking the treasures of the text, when I hit my head on the line: "Let your house be wide open to strangers, treat the

15

poor as members of your own family, and do not gossip with women." The first two sentiments of course were noble, enriching, filling me with the ever-increasing pride I was feeling at the beauty of this tradition. But the third injunction, casually included in such an ethical series, literally knocked the breath out of me. Suddenly, I was "other," in fact, I was the enemy. Moreover, the injunction made clear that my assumption of being addressed, being included by the text, was false, untrue. This was a text written by men, written for men, describing a male religious tradition elucidating subjects of ultimate concern about how men ought to lead their lives and behave in the world.

The sudden recognition of all of this flooded me; I was conscious as well that the insult was not solely an ancient one, but that a continuing line of learned men had failed to edit out the offending sentiment and so had cumulatively added their stamp of approval. I closed the book. The men sitting around the study table with me offered bits of apologetics, none to my mind satisfactory; after a while they tired of this sidetrack we'd gotten off on and so finally, sensing their heightening impatience, I released them to go on to the next verses. But the damage was done. Like suddenly being confronted with incontrovertible proof that a dearly loved and trusted friend was guilty of some truly despicable act, there now was the beginning of a fissure between me and this ancient tradition I had increasingly been cleaving to: I began to ask myself, what was my place in this Jewish world as a woman?

I dealt with my immediate hurt by laying the blame at the feet of the text and it was many years before I again was willing to open the pages of *The Ethics of the Fathers*. But the more I learned, and the more my day to day life became inextricably tied to Jewish tradition, practice, and sensibility, the more I would find myself recycling that question: what was my place in this Jewish world as a woman?

In my senior year of college the Hillel director acquired a new crop of rabbinical students as assistants. Every year several seniors from the Jewish Theological Seminary (the New York institution which trains and ordains Conservative rabbis) came to work as interns at Hillel. Mostly these young men—in those days they were all men—were already married; this year one of them was single: an intense, intellectually keen 24-year-old redhead. What began as a friendship budded into a romance. Since Eddie had compunctions about "dating a student," we agreed I would take none of his classes. Further, we determined our privacy was best served by dating in secret. What that meant in those days in provincial Brooklyn was simply to see each other in Manhattan. Very quickly we came to love each other. A girl who had heard of neither Sukkot nor Shavuot until she was 18 was on her way to becoming a rebbetzin at 20.

Often through the years when people have heard that I grew up in a secular home, they assumed that I "got religion" under the marriage canopy, to please or accommodate my husband the rabbi. Clearly though, I was already well embarked on a spiritual exploration of Judaism when we met. This is not to say however that the Jewish path I continued to travel was unaffected by my travelling companion. Most definitely the contrary was true. I think it would be accurate to say that I continued my search but did so for the next many years on his path. His was the path of someone with a rich and complex family history of observance, someone who was knowledgeable, well educated Jewishly, someone who was religiously sophisticated and destined to participate in shaping a new Jewish future in America.

Eddie and his friends had a difficult time of it at the Seminary. While they received an unparalleled scholarly education there, they longed for a religious environment that could provide community, serious personal interaction with text, social action, and spiritual intensity. They decided to found a new seminary, Havurat Shalom (fellowship of peace), informed by all those ideals and to locate it in the Boston area where some of the central players already lived. Their vision was radical, daring. Their dream was nothing less than the restructuring and rebirth of the American Jewish community.

I had entered the Jewish world at Hillel as a well behaved novice, a sponge. I was uncritical of what I found there for two reasons—one, I was enchanted by the tradition, and two, I didn't know enough to be critical. If I'd grown up in a Jewishly observant home, I probably would have been ripe for rebellion, but in some sense, this entry into Judaism *was* my rebellion. Now suddenly I was in league with a group of people who were enormously sophisticated in their Judaism and ready to make a revolution. I joined them because I was in love and didn't want to be separated from Eddie, because I was excited by their new Jewish venture, and because it was my ticket out of Brooklyn.

# 2

*Beginning Again*

Boston 1968. My first image is the Boston Common on a sunny Sunday afternoon overrun by Hare Krishnas. Tambourines, singing, dancing, flowing white robes, multi-colored scarves . . . Seeing *Casablanca* at the Brattle Theatre . . . Going to hear William Sloan Coffin speak out against the war at the big church off Memorial Drive . . . I remember having cooked my very first meat loaf, going downstairs to the laundromat on the corner, running into some friends and inviting them up for supper. Only after they declined and headed off to their appointment did I realize that so far we only owned two chairs! In those days I suppose we would have just shrugged, declared it a picnic, and settled in on the floor.

We were poor but it was the poverty of graduate students, play-poverty, poverty to last for a while and then be nostalgic about years later. Eddie taught Hebrew school; I started out as a parttime clerk at Boston Children's Hospital, then spent most of the year subbing in the Boston school system. A clerk from the School Committee office would call you before eight in the morning, tell you what class you had ("K through 12") and where in the city the school was located. Using a fat little booklet published by the School Committee, you looked up the school you had been assigned, followed the directions from Park Street on the T and spent the day taking the abuse you remembered giving subs when you were a kid. Mostly I was in way over my head—often, subbing in a high school, I would be stopped in the hall by other teachers, mistaken for a student and scolded for being out of class without a pass. Once I had a totally out of control kindergarten class and, at my wit's end, took them out to the playground for the last half hour of the day. Some of the boys decided that even more fun than trying to kill each other would be to queue up at one wall of the school building, unzip their pants and see who could pee the furthest. There I was, running up and down this line of 5 year olds, sternly commanding, "You put that back!" At three o'clock I'd crawl home, cry for an hour or so and then make tuna casserole for supper.

Seven men were the founders and teachers of Havurat Shalom, begun in Cambridge in the summer of 1968. There

21

were about fifteen formally enrolled students, also all men. One of the important guiding principles of this new seminary community was to break down or minimize the distinctions between faculty and students, e.g., decisions were not imposed from above by the faculty, rather, faculty and students all gathered at weekly community meetings and either everyone voted or talked well into the night until we reached consensus. (We were very big on consensus. Acting like Quakers seemed to be a particular pleasure for Jews of our generation.)

The ethos of equality was powerful; in fact, there was serious discussion about whether faculty members should also pay the $500 annual tuition. What was finally agreed upon was that students would pay, the money would help to cover costs for the building, and faculty members would teach without salary. That selflessness and idealism moves me even more today than it did back then. Nowadays when friends have a dream of a new Jewish institution, we turn on our computers and put in a hard day of grantwriting. Then of course we had the luxury of being young, without families, and with nothing to lose. But still I feel sentimental about having been part of a time and a generation that believed in its causes so passionately, it didn't mind fighting for them till it hurt; in fact I think the "hurting" was a not incidental part of the passion, to be poor in the service of a great cause.

The only women who were associated with Havurat Shalom at its inception were the wives and girlfriends of the faculty and students—we were adjuncts. We women were free to take courses with the students, although classes met during the day and most of us were otherwise occupied. We participated in communal meals, in *davenning* (prayer services) and in group discussions. We could speak out at community meetings but we did not have a vote.

I think it crucial that we women were not involved in this community because of a clear individual volitional decision to be, but rather for affiliative reasons. It seems to me that how and why group members come to find themselves in a group

22

has a lot to do with what they expect and what is expected of them by way of participation in that group. Before the advent of the women's liberation movement, I suspect many women found themselves in groups for what were originally affiliative reasons and that we all failed to see the significance of that— when it is your vision, your passion, your disaffection which has impelled you to strike out on a new path, of course you will think it right and proper that you have a voice in how to chart the course, how to ration the food and water; if you started out on the journey simply to spend an afternoon with your boyfriend, you stand to the side, a bit in back, when decisions are to be made.

The women. We were included and yet we weren't included. We were valued for our company, our insights, and our cooking. Yet there was a silent wall that held us back. Our ignorance? Our timidity? The insensitivity or prejudice of the men? Our peripheral status, our totally unclear role in the life of the community? To be fair all around, neither the young men nor the young women who participated in the founding of Havurat Shalom, the cornerstone of the Jewish renewal movement, had any role models for the equal participation of women in the Jewish community.

I think it not incidental that the popular subject of study at Havurat Shalom was of Hasidism, of Buber and Rosensweig. Both the Hasidic and the German Jewish writers celebrated direct, unmediated spiritual experience; both cultures questioned the authority of the Talmud and the rabbis. They promulgated revolutionary attitudes, which valued the spiritual life of the common [man], which dared to suggest that the uninitiated could also study biblical texts. I wonder now what the subliminal effect of that study was on us: Did it empower the students, did it empower the women, to begin to think of themselves and each other as equal to their teachers?

What was the role of the women in Shabbat services, a centrally important group activity? I honestly don't remember if we were counted in the minyan or not. The room was always

23

full and we didn't seem ever to need to wait for a minyan. Did the women lead parts of the service? Little or not at all as I recall—it would have been difficult to gather together a more impressive, more intimidating group of men, and we women were either lacking Jewish education, were temperamentally reserved, or both. I'm sure I wasn't the only one who felt awed simply to be in the room. Like most women in 1968, my consciousness had yet to be raised. The very factors that kept us, as women, on the periphery of the community were the issues we were just beginning to explore as nascent feminists. They came, as all human truths do, through the mundane, the everyday.

We were all away together on retreat, had eaten a big meal, and although most people helped to clear the table, the men then rushed into the meeting room to continue whatever deep spiritual discussion we were in the midst of. Faced with a cleanup for over twenty people, I exploded at the two least threatening students in the group. Hadn't everyone eaten? Who were we women, the servants? I think that, most importantly, this incident reminds me how men and women at that time were just beginning to learn together what sexism was, were thinking with a sudden urgency that old patterns and attitudes might undermine a contemporary Jewish utopia, that to radicalize and empower a passive, rabbi-centered American Jewish community also implied breaking down the hierarchies that sexism imposed.

During the public reading of the Torah, on Shabbat, on holidays, and at other prescribed times, members of the congregation are "called up" to the Torah (the Hebrew for this, *aliya,* means literally "to go up") and before and after the Hebrew verses are chanted from the scroll, the designated person recites a blessing and in doing so is honored. Until this generation, those honors were reserved exclusively for men. The first time a woman had an *aliya* at Havurat Shalom was in May 1969, as part of a couple—one of the students was about to be married and so he and his wife-to-be were called up to the Torah together. We did it that way because it seemed like the most natural way to celebrate. I don't think prior to that moment it had occurred to any of us that women were being excluded. Once having done it though, there was no going back—it suddenly seemed obvious that women should be honored with *aliyot*, and not only as a part of a couple and not only to celebrate an impending marriage.

We were young; we made changes as we went along, as fallible men and women honestly confronting ourselves, each other and the Jewish tradition we saw ourselves as bringing to new life. The story of the women of Havurat Shalom in that first year is the story of women everywhere at the onset of the feminist movement. What we had to conquer before any of the external work of liberation could begin was the deeply ingrained self-image of being less than the men we loved and with whom we worked. Our liberation had to begin with our own questioning of the status quo, with our own assertion of our dignity and worth.

July 1969. The first time I saw Champaign-Urbana, Eddie had already been hired as director of the University of Illinois Hillel Foundation. We flew out on Ozark Airlines; I was fascinated by the bird's eye view of the checkerboard pattern of Midwestern farms below us—180 acre land grant farms, each with a house and barn in one corner of the property. An austere life, I thought, each family on its own. We landed at the airport and deplaned at gate three—literally a chain link fence and gate with a small painted sign, "gate 3." (One Thanksgiving weekend there were actually two planes preparing for takeoff at the same time. Great confusion, great excitement.)

We entered the small terminal and approached the Hertz desk to rent a car: we had come for a few days to look for a place to live. The woman at the counter asked, "Do you work for an organization that gets one of our discounts?" She looked up "B'nai B'rith," and sure enough, we qualified; she proceeded to fill out the necessary form. "What's your job title?"

she asked Eddie. "Rabbi," he replied. Her response—"What's a rabbi?" Well, I thought, this is an adventure . . . (For a number of years thereafter, when someone asked what my husband's profession was, I would say, "He's a Jewish minister.")

For the actual move to Champaign we decided to take the train. We wanted a way to reinforce the reality that we were moving and that it was in fact a considerable distance, that we were going to a different part of the country yet it was still a part of the country we knew. If you get on a plane, we reasoned, it's somehow all the same, you pass the time, then you arrive. You don't have a real sense of the distance. So we took the train. My mother, Eddie's brother and sister-in-law came to see us off. It was hard to separate, but exciting to be going. After we left, Marcia said she and my mother cried. "They're so young!" Young we were, especially me. I remember thinking, how strange the world is—I've known this man for a year and a half and here I am saying goodbye to my family, to all my friends, starting a new life with him alone.

We rented a duplex apartment in a new development at the edge of the cornfields. We spent the next few weeks settling in, buying a car, discovering the wonders of a Midwestern invention called K-Mart, finding the local supermarkets, setting up a kosher kitchen, creating bookcases and a coffee table out of bricks and boards. We got dining room chairs at a second hand store, I painted them a shiny bright red enamel. The old oak rocker we spent a year stripping. And then the first day of the university school year and Eddie set out in the morning for work. I sat in that apartment looking around at the red enamel chairs, the brick and board bookcases, the flat cornfield vistas out the window and I suddenly realized, I don't know what I'm doing with the rest of my life. I'm 21 years old, it's 1969, this is the scene after they ride off into the sunset together, happily ever after. And I don't know what I'm supposed to do today. Or tomorrow. Or two years from now. I don't know. And I don't know what I want. And furthermore, who is it who's asking these questions? This young woman, who is she?

The years of my childhood and adolescence were taken up with survival. I went to school, I studied hard, I got good grades, I had parttime jobs, most of all I struggled to keep my head above the quicksand of depression in my home. I knew what it was I wanted out of—I wanted out of that apartment, I wanted out of provincial Brooklyn. In other words, I knew what I didn't want. But what was it I did want? It was only in my twenties that I finally had the opportunity and the psychic energy to begin exploring that question.

I knew I wasn't ready for children and so I managed to sidestep the occasional inquiry about when they might be coming. Not being much of a materialist, it had seemed to me that Eddie was making more than enough money for our modest needs, so I felt no real economic incentive to work. Suddenly though, for the first time in my life, my days were empty. I first took a job in a dress shop, just to keep busy, to have some social interaction during the day, to have some destination, a structure. Pretty quickly though the routine of arranging racks of little skirts and sweaters from lighter to ever darker solids, followed on the racks by prints and patterns— pretty quickly those routines grew boring and I was lucky to find a job as a technical writer at the National Council of Teachers of English which happened to have its national head- quarters in Champaign-Urbana. Soon I was also a student again, in graduate school—I missed the discipline and companion- ship of studying literature with other students and with a teacher. By the fourth year I was teaching freshman composi- tion, stimulated by what I experienced as my first real chal- lenge in the world of work.

But the focus here is the first year—not only the first year as a working adult, but the first year of marriage, the first year as a wife. Living day in day out with another person, a person who left his underwear wherever he happened to have taken it off, a person who woke up slowly, later in the morning, and made it clear he did not appreciate my singing around the house before he'd had a first cup of coffee and cigarette. A person who came home from work at the end of the day asking what's for supper and who finally became angry with the response, "I don't know, I forgot to defrost." He didn't want to eat out every night, he didn't like dustballs in the bedroom. It was 1969 and he wanted a wife. But as little as I knew about the world or myself, I knew I didn't want to play Lillian to anyone's Milton. Playing Lillian meant you gave endlessly and you got what in return? The chance to get up tomorrow and give more. No, I don't think so.

In the first year of marriage, the fact that we were friends and lovers was often of the dimmest significance. Frequently at the fore was a raging battle over what "wife" and "husband" meant to me, what "wife" and "husband" meant to him, what our expectations of the other were, what our emotional baggage vis-à-vis those roles was and the fighting fury to avoid whatever position seemed at the moment to smell of victim. When you marry young, it takes a long time just to realize what it is you're really fighting about—it's not about the garbage, it's not about the steak you didn't get defrosted in time for dinner, it's not about dustballs on the bedroom floor. It's more likely about *do you respect me or am I going to get walked all over here*, it's probably about *you didn't hear me, you don't listen, you don't take the time to understand me, you didn't respond in a way that feels good* . . . Not much time or energy that first year to reflect on how is this home Jewish, what do we each want from a Jewish home, how do you create a Jewish home . . . So few people manage to stay together, both of them still alive inside, alive to each other, willing to struggle to understand, to talk or fight their way through differences, pain, miscommunication to get to the other side where there's pleasure, ease, warmth, sharing, that the determination to keep at it feels like a miracle in our time. It's becoming an unusual spiritual expression for us as moderns—to stay in a marriage, weather the storms, remain open to the possibility of falling in love all over again with the same person you started out with. A modern miracle.

The years in the Midwest radicalized me in slow motion. (Actually, to a New Yorker, everything in the Midwest seems to happen in slow motion. Some easterners are driven mad by that, others, like me, are charmed, grateful to slow down, grateful even for the sudden absence of mountain, absence of ocean, forcing us to slow down, look up, notice the landscape of sky, clouds, stars.) So I slowed down, I got into *pleasant, polite.* Strangers saying "good morning" when they passed you on the street, salespeople genuinely trying to be helpful. Once at an anti-war rally that started on campus and moved to the sleepy center of downtown, the frenzy built to an explosive pitch when finally Harvey Shirley, the local chief of police, picked up a bullhorn and announced calmly, matter-of-factly, "I don't know about all you folks, but I'm tired now, it's late, and I'm going home." The phalanx of National Guardsmen retreated, the crowd dispersed.

The only Shabbat morning services on campus were Orthodox. Unlike my experience at Brooklyn College Hillel or at Havurat Shalom, the room wasn't crowded, every week there was a struggle to get a minyan. Every week one of the graduate students, one of the observant young faculty members, one of the undergraduate boys, would stand at the front of the sanctuary and count with his finger, "one, two, three . . . seven . . . " His finger never wandered over to the other side of the *meḥitza.* Inevitably, especially on those cold winter mornings when ice storms made the long walk to shul treacherous, inevitably there would come the request, "Someone call Jay." Since traditional Jews consider use of the phone a violation of Shabbat, there's a large irony in the request to make a call on Shabbat to get a quorum for Orthodox prayer. Nevertheless, the member of the group who had the least compunctions about using the phone would wake up poor Jay, or Howie, or Murray, roust the unfortunate good citizen out of his warm bed to make a minyan.

Slowly, slowly, those cold Shabbos mornings radicalized me, helped to transform me into a Jewish feminist (not that there

29

was such a category at the time—the category came after). On those cold mornings I thought, I'm sitting here, I walked all the way, my face and shoulders parting the icy winds, but now as I sit here, waiting to pray, I am invisible, worthless, I am as if I had stayed home cozy under the covers. "Someone call Jay." It didn't start with my needing an honor, needing to lead part of the service, needing to be called up to the Torah for an aliya (though later, on Simchas Torah, the holiday which celebrates completing and beginning again the yearly cycle of reading the Torah, when traditionally every Jew present has the honor of an aliya, on Simchas Torah one year in Champaign when someone repeatedly bellowed from the front, peering out at the raucous holiday crowd, "Is there *anyone* who hasn't had an aliya yet?" I raised my hand, I waved my arms, I made a spectacle of myself . . . ) But it didn't start with wanting an honor, it started with just wanting to be counted as one of ten Jewish adults to make up the quorum for prayer. It started with "Someone call Jay."

One year in Champaign, for Purim, when everyone is supposed to dress up in costume and an assortment of ages and sizes of Queen Esthers abound, I dressed as Vashti and sat outside the service with a picket sign and petition, gathering signatures to protest the unfair treatment of the King's first wife, punished because she refused to do the drunken King's bidding and dance naked before his court. But that was fun, that was tongue-in-cheek, that was really in keeping with the carnival spirit of the holiday. In fact, that was easy precisely because I could find within the holiday a creative outlet for my righteous anger. But Purim comes once a year, Simchas Torah comes once a year: Shabbat services were a fixture in my week. "Someone call Jay."

Eddie and I found a few kindred spirits and together we organized an alternative Shabbos morning minyan. We chanted some of the prayers in English, we had intense discussions of the biblical portion of the week, we counted Jewish women equally with Jewish men in the quorum for prayer. On a campus with three thousand Jewish students, we often squeaked by with only ten or eleven present, sometimes we didn't make it to ten. In those days, in the late '60s, early '70s, it was overwhelmingly the case that the observant Jewish women I knew wanted nothing to do with feminism, and the feminists I knew ran as far away as they could get from their Jewish identity. For two years Eddie tried to get a woman undergraduate/graduate student/faculty member/community person to accept an aliya at the vast Conservative high holiday service at Hillel. It took him three years to find a woman willing to dare it.

I was lonely, terribly lonely. How could it be I cared so much about something half the Jewish population was hostile to and the other half viewed with indifference? My only real support, beyond Eddie, was from the wives of some of his colleagues. In those days most Hillel directors were rabbis, all rabbis were men, virtually all Hillel directors were men. Though they came from all the Jewish denominations and so represented the fullest spectrum of Jewish life, a delightful and dizzying smorgasbord of belief and practice, what they had in common was an independence of spirit and intellect—they were mavericks each in his own movement and frequently married to women who also saw things from a unique perspective. Once or twice a year, we would gather from all corners of the country for professional conferences. The women, who often were unpaid partners in their husbands' campus work, would come along to enjoy the fellowship and support of being with people they rarely saw but who knew each other's intimate pains and joys almost before they were spoken. Especially crucial were the December gatherings, which in those days took place at Grossingers (we were a passionate bunch—the only group ever to come to the most famous of the Borscht Belt hotels and stage a hunger strike protesting their obscene waste of food while famine raged abroad). We women organized official and unofficial conferences parallel to the professional meetings taking place in the rooms down the hall; we shared in the birth pangs of Jewish feminism, explored the limits of Jewish law in regard to women and challenged each other's imaginations to discover how those limits could be stretched, pushed, moved, reexamined. These rebbetzins—Esther Ticktin, Rachel Adler, Ruthie Polak, Mara Poupko, Ann Fisher, Ellie Levine, to name a few—these were the women who understood my pain at not having a place at the table, who didn't think I was strange for wanting a place at the table. They wanted a place too. We dared to ask questions and answer them in a more forceful and radical way than our local communities were ready to hear. From widely varying backgrounds and stages of life, we came together and helped in ways large and small to make a revolution. We needed each other, we loved each other, we strengthened each other. And then we returned home, each to her own campus, challenging students to question, to celebrate, to demand dignity, education, and equality for Jewish women.

During the spring of our fourth and last year in Champaign, the first Jewish women's conference was organized to take place in New York. I knew many of the women who had worked on planning it, I knew many of the women who would be speaking at this historic event, I felt tremendous excitement that such a gathering was taking place, I longed to be there, to be one of them, to see, to hear, to be counted. I didn't go. I couldn't go. I couldn't bring myself to spend the money on the airfare for something for me. I was working, Eddie was working, we had no extraordinary expenses at the time: as I look back on it, it's clear to me that the problem wasn't truly a budgetary one, the problem was in my mind, the problem was spiritual. I had been brought up to be tightfisted, with the unspoken cardinal rule which clearly applied to my mother and which I understood by extension to apply as well to me—don't spend money on yourself.

Other childhood memories, not the sun-filled ones, not the grandmother ones, not the safe and happy ones: my short mother, on her short legs, running, always running, pulling a heavy shopping cart from the store with the cheapest dairy to the store with the cheapest canned goods, washing clothes by hand for a family of five, waiting in the early morning hours for some school to call, "Mrs. Lewis, we need a sub today." Heavy unspoken tension if the phone didn't ring, all the while she and we pretending the money wasn't needed for the gas bill, wasn't needed for groceries, for rent.

Waking in the cold, in the dark, in the middle of winter nights, my bladder full, desperate for the bathroom, afraid to get out of bed and run the gauntlet of cockroaches.

Sharing a tiny bedroom with my older brother until he was 17 and I was 15, with another older brother sleeping on the living room couch—not one of those cute fold-out couches the little girl with blond ringlets demonstrated on TV—just a regular couch with a sheet brought out from the closet every night.

Sharing a tiny bedroom with my older brother until he was 17 and I was 15, every morning and every night getting undressed and dressed—quickly, quickly—someone's coming—when was the first time I saw my own naked body in a full-length mirror? I must have been twenty years old. Getting dressed and undressed—quickly, quickly—my brothers teasing on the other side of the door as they waited their turn to dress.

A softer memory, one I can smile at now—how quietly can you give yourself pleasure when you're sharing the room with an older brother? I learned to be oh so quiet.

And what about being Jewish when there's no money in the house? You don't join, you can't afford to join. No synagogue for us on the High Holidays—if you need your money for food you can't spend it on High Holiday tickets. We sneak in to say Yizkor, we dress up and sit in the living room and call

33

it Rosh Hashanah. Hadassah for Mom? No money for the little outfits, for the luncheons, for the raffle books. And how could *we* invite *them* to *our* home?

Only relatives come into our home. No friends, no neighbors, no children from class, no birthday parties. Two hundred Crown Street, that has a nice sound to it, but people can't come inside to see how we live, how tiny, how old, how worn the furniture. There are no pictures of 200 Crown Street—when we took pictures, we always used other buildings on the block as a backdrop. Funny, when it was time for family pictures, how the sun was never in the right place in front of our building.

The world outside: the pain of watching TV, the pain of comparing ourselves to that house, that family on *Father Knows Best*, the pain, the shame. Why couldn't we do what they made it look so easy to do—to have a pretty house, a white picket fence. They made it look easy to succeed in America, but we weren't succeeding, we were failures. We were that other TV family, we were *The Honeymooners*. Shame and secrecy and pretense and false pride.

Margaret, my best friend who lived in one of the private houses that lined our street, Margaret:

"Merle, let's go—"
"No Margaret, I don't feel like it."
"Oh Merle, you always say no, why don't you ever want to try something new?"

What could I say? Because I'm afraid it will cost money? Because in my small world I don't know enough to know what costs money and what's free for the taking? Margaret:

"Why don't you at least *ask* your mother if you can go?"

What could I say? It hurts too much to see the sadness come across her face as she makes up some excuse? She never says, "No, because we can't afford it Merle."

What did I learn from my childhood?

Don't ask for what you can't have.
Try not to want what you can't have.
Try not to want anything very much.

The good woman puts her needs last.

Dreams are permitted small children.
Dreaming is too dangerous for adults (adults who have no advantages).
Dreaming is for someone else.
Dreaming is for Margaret.

Why write these things, why share these things, why bring them to the surface? They're painful and shameful, better forgotten. But if we want to speak of the life of spirit we cannot pretend that money and class do not impinge mightily on that life. Some of us aren't there to be counted on Yom Kippur because we don't have the money for tickets. So there we are on the outside, looking in. And of course the life of spirit is not limited to the confines of the local sanctuary—a thin purse or a background unfamiliar with a rich cultural vocabulary can also deprive us of the nourishment of ballet, of symphony, of sculpture, of theater.

And even the spiritual food of light and sky, the color green, the pounding of the surf, even these necessities which nourish the soul are hard to access when you're poor, when you don't own a car, when you're uncertain about which pleasures cost money and which pleasures are free for the taking. You stay home rather than embarrass yourself by showing up someplace you don't belong.

Everything in our culture tells us, if you can't afford it, you are unworthy, you are inferior. Today, now, even in secular America, even in Jewish America, Calvin lives: you know if you don't have money, this is proof that you are unworthy. You know it. When you're poor, you have all the pain and fear of being poor, and on top of that, you live apart from any warmth, from any hope, that the community could provide. You live in isolation and in shame.

The truth is that, more often than not, growing up in poverty shrinks the spirit, makes us believe we are somehow not deserving of the range of pleasures that money can buy. Even a pleasure as singular as flying a thousand miles to attend a watershed conference for Jewish feminists.

What is the power of a poet? The power to tell a new story, or an old story in a new way that allows one to hear. So here's a story.

When I was a child—I don't think I could have been more than five, and Roger then maybe seven or eight—my mother got a new clothes hamper. I don't really remember the old one, but it must have been beyond repair for my mother to have allowed herself a new one. It was winter, a snowy winter, the hamper was then perhaps a week or two old, and Roger, always a curious boy with an experimental bent, apparently began to wonder if snow would burn. So he scraped some snow off the windowsill and snuck it into the only private space we all had—the bathroom. Then he lit a match, or I suppose, a number of matches. Of course he didn't manage to "burn" the snow, but he did manage to set fire to the lid of the new hamper. When the excitement died down and Roger had been lectured on children playing with matches, my mother produced a bit of floral contact paper and quietly recovered the now charred and ugly lid of her new hamper. Every year or two after that when she was recovering a kitchen counter or the seat of the kitchen step stool, the hamper would get spruced up again as well. My mother was very good with contact paper.

What is this story doing in this book, a book about spirituality, about Jewish feminist spirituality? Well, this is a book that tells what I know about the life of spirit, how I've searched for it, how I've found it and lost it, been wounded and been nourished. What makes spirit grow, what shrivels it. My mother loved Roger with all her heart, and she wasn't the type to bear a grudge anyway, so for her and for him the story of the hamper became one of those classic stories that tell something important and funny and slightly embarrassing about what you once did as a kid. But for me, an observer and not a player in this drama, it taught a different lesson. The hamper was something you had wanted, a small thing really, but you wanted it and it gave you pleasure and then it was ruined and you didn't have the power to replace it, to wipe away the injury and forget it. You were stuck with it in its ruined state and three or four times a day when you went into that small bathroom, right in front of you was that scarred hamper, its ugliness contact papered over, but there underneath just the same, a reminder that taking pleasure in even the smallest luxury made you vulnerable. The pleasure was fleeting, the disappointment lasting. The lesson? Want little, buy less, control your needs, contain your needs. Not that it works, not that you can do that really—those impulses will break through any way they can—but the impulse is a vise around the spirit, whispering: make your needs small, make yourself small. You have no power, you know nothing of power. You're not powerful enough to fix anything, to change anything. Know your place, stay in your place. The lesson of poverty. Death to spirit.

A few years ago my friend Marty brought the house down with her opening words in a keynote address to the plenary session of a prestigious women's conference. She began her talk by announcing to the assembled intellectual elite that when invited to give the keynote, her greatest difficulty had not been choosing a topic, nor reworking her demanding schedule, not the process of writing the talk, not even the contemplation of effective delivery. Her only real concern had been deciding what to wear. After waiting a good while for the appreciative laughter of audience self-recognition to subside, she then detailed each possibility of her wardrobe and shared her assessment of the subtle nuances which one after another potential outfits would have communicated about her.

What I remember most vividly about our visit to Princeton in the spring of 1973 when Eddie interviewed for the position of Hillel director at the university was my agitation about what I should wear. I even went so far as to quiz a friend in the Hillel National Office (who had just come from Princeton where he'd consulted with some of the people we'd be meeting there) to ask him what the women had worn. He seemed taken aback by my question, thought a moment or two and said, there were no adult women on the search committee, only one or two undergraduates. Oh yes, he added, there was a university secretary present, but she had been dressed like a secretary. Until that moment (I was only 24), I had never considered that secretaries had a unique costume code (presumably, I inferred from his tone, undesirable) and now my stomach knotted several more times as I contemplated that I might show up for Eddie's interview at this Ivy League college unwittingly dressed like a secretary.

In those bygone days it seemed the fashion in Princeton, at least for some, to be purposely vague about practical matters, almost as if by being clear and straightforward you were showing yourself to be ordinary—the true genius should be distracted, above such mundane matters as imparting instructions, directions. (In those years none of the campus buildings had signs with their names on them—an affectation that seemed to signal, if you don't know where you are, you don't belong here.) Whatever the cause, the person who gave us driving directions to get to town for Eddie's interview said to take Route 206 and then vaguely trailed off with, "when you hit the main drag you'll know it, the campus will be obvious, just park and ask a passerby to point you to the right building." Back and forth we drove on Route 206, our alarm and then panic mounting as the appointed hour for the first meeting drew ever nearer, each time unknowingly sideswiping the town and the campus at its center. Back and forth, back and forth we drove, it's got to be here somewhere. Finally we swallowed our pride, pulled into a roadside convenience store and were told by a local merchant how to get to Nassau Street.

The interview process took a few days; for some of the meetings my presence was requested, for others not. I walked the campus, walked the streets of the too charming downtown and wondered if I could ever fit in here, ever feel at home. Could I be happy here, could I be myself? If I couldn't be myself, I knew I couldn't be happy and so wouldn't want to come. I kept looking around and wondering, can I wear jeans here? If I can't feel at ease wearing jeans here, this won't work.

The jeans were in fact a very real issue. That's what I wore and wear, most of the time—my friend Frima once dryly responded when I asked her advice on an appropriate outfit for a fancy reception I was obliged to attend, "What can I suggest to a woman who wore a jean skirt to her son's bris!" (In my own defense, I figured the fact that it was a skirt made it dressier, and I was thrilled at that point to fit into anything with a waist.) But the jeans were also of course a symptom, a symbol. My liabilities were clear to me: a Brooklyn accent, a diploma from Brooklyn College, a manner and a way of being in the world which was straightforward, unassuming, warm and frank, ethnically unquestionably undeniably Jewish. I no sooner considered changing or concealing any of that than I had ever for more than ten minutes in junior high school contemplated having a nose job. The question wasn't what could I or should I do about these cultural and class liabilities of mine, the question was, could I find a place for myself in this quintessentially WASP world? Eddie wanted the job, I decided to give it a try. We stayed 19 years.

Like most of the Ivies, Princeton had a history of anti-Semitism, a history which the university administration that was in place when we arrived found morally unacceptable, unworthy of a great institution of higher learning. But the history was there and ghosts remained. I remember in our early years welcoming into Hillel a freshman from New Jersey, a short dark boy who looked unmistakably Jewish and who a few weeks into his first semester affected a British accent which he maintained for the four years till he graduated. I don't know that I want to call that self-hatred, somehow the word feels too violent, though it was violence he did to himself through that act, but I certainly saw it as a profound rejection of self. And that was what I saw as our role at Princeton in creating a Hillel Foundation—I viewed us as being engaged in guerilla warfare for the souls of Jewish students in this WASP, high brow, disapproving Ivy League culture. We would be models not only of Jewish intellectual inquiry, spiritual curiosity and depth, but also of Jewish self-acceptance, Jewish self-love, in an environment that still in those days was judgmental, critical, rejecting of many particularities. (In the 1996 edition of *The Best 309 Colleges*, a volume I just happen to have lying around the house from my daughter's senior year in high school, the writer remarks that a quarter of Princeton's students are minorities: "Wrote one Hispanic student, 'If you are a minority, you must come here.'") But in 1973, Jewish students on their way to Rosh Hashana services on campus covered their holiday suits and ties with trench coats to avoid attracting unwanted attention.

Because I lived in Princeton in an era that increasingly told women not to be adjuncts to their husband's lives, and because I in fact always had a rich and complicated life independent of Eddie and his work, and because as well I was never a paid employee of Princeton Hillel, I really did not acknowledge to others or to myself how central my Hillel involvement was to me. But it was. Before I was mother to Lisa and Uri, and even after, I was mother to generations of Princeton undergraduates. I used to joke I practiced on them, I used to say I had all the advantages of their adolescent energy around the house without bearing the brunt of their adolescent rebellion or getting their tuition bills in the mail. I joked, but their presence in my life was precious to me. Feeding them, listening to their heartaches, watching them develop, mature, become strong and whole, was a joy that filled me until I cried as they received their diplomas and long after that as they returned to my home as peers and friends.

The creation of a home and the act of nourishing the people who live in and visit that home has a spiritual force that the devotees of Martha Stewart both sense and miss as surely as Eddie and I missed the turnoff for Princeton proper driving in for our first interview. The yearning to surround yourself and your dear ones with what you've made from scratch, by hand—food, decor, clothing—is a yearning to nurture and caress the spirit, the soul, the innermost tender being of the other. Indisputably, when forced upon us, this role of nurturer, of homemaker, is not a gift of spirit, but rather death to spirit. When it is imposed on us because we happen to be women and that has always been the lot of women, when it demands our constant and undivided attention, it robs us of the opportunity to live and grow in other ways—one day a year may be enough to declare the legal status of a road, but it's not enough for a human being to say, "I belong to myself." The gifts of one's time and energy and creativity must be free will offerings; then and only then can domestic activities be wellsprings of spiritual power. We as feminists have fought the restrictive understandings of women's roles in order to liberate women as full human beings; perhaps now though we have reached a time and place where we can reclaim the possibility of domestic life as humanly fulfilling, enriching.

During the years in Champaign, during the years in Princeton, I created a home which let in the light and into that home I welcomed Jewish students. I didn't cook and bake and schlep because my husband demanded it or because my role demanded it—I would never have allowed any such demand to be imposed on me. I did it freely, joyously, I did it because it satisfied one aspect of my spiritual longings. It was work that was as defining of my sense of self and sense of meaning as writing a play, putting together a poetry reading, teaching a class or delivering a talk. Even the process was not all that different: creative engagement, careful planning, methodical attention to every detail, unstinting hard work, and then, when the lights come up on stage, letting go of it all, giving up control, stepping aside and allowing whatever needs to happen to happen, taking a leap of faith which permits the spirit to soar.

A case in point, the seder. The work begins a week or two before Pesach. Brutal physical labor which drained me even as a twentysomething. Spring cleaning with a vengeance. Starting from the farthest corners of the house, scrubbing, serious scrubbing, down on your hands and knees, emptying the backs of closets, overturning, rearranging, polishing, cleaning like a person possessed, then finally entering the eye of the storm, the kitchen itself. Nothing is safe, the normal year-round order completely overturned. The food in the pantry must go, the regular dishes, the regular pots and pans must go; the refrigerator, the stove, must gleam, even cleaner than for snoopy in-laws, even cleaner than for resale—clean enough for God. Rational sense it doesn't make, it's tradition, so you do it. Then the schlepping, of meat, of fish, of dairy, of vegetables. Many pounds of onions, many pounds of mushrooms, of lettuce, of carrots, of celery, of tomatoes, broccoli, squash, potatoes, radishes . . . from the grocery to the car, from the car to the kitchen, I am so tired, all I can think is lettuce, onions, no part of me doesn't ache, what did you have in mind God? Then you're going down the home stretch: cooking, cooking, set the table, Eddie's grating horseradish, the guests are at the door.

Over the years we found a rhythm that accommodated communal obligation and personal longing: the first seder usually necessitated our being at the kosher dining hall with Eddie officiating; the second night we were at home. The guest list was limited to about fourteen, the greatest number our small dining room could hold, still intimate enough for community. Each guest was asked to bring a question, preferably, though not necessarily, one related to Passover. Once a year this opportunity to sit with students who were especial favorites and often far from home, with stranded foreign visitors, with childhood playmates, with faculty going through a bad divorce, with neighbors who had only just gotten up from sitting shiva. We'd sit and talk about the meaning of our lives, our search for freedom, our yearning to live in a redeemed world. Never did we get to the food before 11:30 at night, rarely was the reward for a stolen afikomen negotiated before one in the morning. We'd sing, we'd sing, then fling open the door for Elijah. One year, long long ago, a particularly precious memory for me: Eddie related the custom of some Sephardic Jews to sit through the seder with a knapsack of matzah on their backs, as if ready to "go out from Egypt" at a moment's notice; then these Sephardim would symbolically walk the borders of their town, carrying their matzah as they went. Sara, a beautiful student (who was then perhaps a sophomore, now long since a professor of mathematics at an Israeli university where she lives with her husband and I believe four children) exclaimed with frustration, "We always *talk* about such things, why can't we ever *do* them?!" So up we all got, all fourteen of us, and walked the staid streets of Princeton in the dark, singing, carrying our matzah in our hands, spirits soaring.

It would be hard to single out my favorite holiday, but if pressed I would probably declare Sukkoth to be most joyous. It comes in the fall, at harvest time. If you're lucky enough to have a backyard, or some scrap of land at your disposal, you build a little harvest booth: ours was a wooden frame designed by Eddie, with old Indian bedspreads for walls. On top of this little playhouse stretched stalks of corn, hanging crook neck gourds and strings of cranberries. Run a utility cord from the house, screw in a yellow bug light for the evening meals, and you're ready to eat in this little booth for the eight days of the holiday. Hillel students and friends and nursery school classes and Christian neighbors—who could keep track of all the people who ate in that sukkah for eight lunches and suppers, snacks and afternoon teas, a week each year for nineteen years. (One particular memory: the first time I ever invited my then playwriting teacher home to dinner, it happened to be—an accident?—during the week of Sukkoth. He reported later his wonder at gaining entrance through a seemingly normal looking front door, being led through a perfectly respectable dining room, then out to the backyard to eat in a hut that swayed gently in the night air and boasted a decor of Indian corn dangling above our heads. Though he'd long since lost most memory of Jewish blood flowing through his veins, he understood at that moment that Eddie and I were his soulmates.)

Why is a sukkah so magical to me? It's the essence of my home, the play-home, even better than the real home, to invite people into. It's a promise—come to my sukkah, come to my play-home tonight and I will make you happy. We will play by my rules, and cruelty and falsity are outlawed. Together we will cast a spell, just for the evening, and everyone at the table will add their softness, their laughter, their sweetness, their songs, and we will play together as if of course the world has meaning and it will all turn out right in the end and we will have fun and no one can hurt us here in this magical play-home.

But Sukkoth comes only once a year, Passover comes only once a year, Shabbat is a weekly opportunity for creation. When I say Shabbat in this context, I don't mean the entire twenty-five hour period from sunset Friday to sunset Saturday. I really mean Friday night.

In a sense preparation for Shabbat begins whenever I call guests to invite them for dinner, that could be a week or two ahead, perhaps only a few days ahead. The actual work begins though when I bake the challah. I started baking my own challah in 1969 as a bride living in a small town in central Illinois which had no kosher bakery, the only available bread being supermarket loaves all of which boasted "animal fat" in the list of ingredients, a shortening which rendered them not kosher. But long after I moved to locales that had tasty kosher bread readily available I continued baking my own challah. Quite simply, I am putting something of me in the bread—my time, my effort, my energy, my love even. I mix it, it rises, I punch it down, I add the raisins, I braid it, it rises. Then I dip my fingers in beaten egg, smooth them across the braided top, sprinkle on poppy seeds or sesame. I break off a little piece of dough, say the blessing, put the trays in the oven. The smell fills the house, fills the hearts of my children, it goes beyond cooking. I can't stay in a bad mood making challah, it soothes me, it calms me, it puts my life in perspective. Bread on its way to a holy moment. I always feel that when the challah is done, many braided loaves snuggled against each other, I'm more than halfway home to having the Shabbos dinner ready.

But of course I make and serve more than the challah. By Wednesday night, 11:00, standing barefoot in the kitchen, I'm planning a menu, writing out a shopping list. Thursday, before work, after work, there's the marketing to be done, the shlepping. Buy enough, make enough, so that if unexpected additional guests turn up, I can always say, yes, please come, it's fine, there's plenty to eat. Thursday night, or Friday morning, I'm cooking. After the challah, my next priority is soup. If the soup is done, I feel I'm three quarters of the way home. Finally, a main course, side dishes, dessert. The food is ready, I set the table. Simple, because simple has always pleased me most. I dim the lights in the room, quite literally setting the scene for the ancient ritual which is about to unfold in my home.

The holiest time of the week for me is Friday night, the holiest moment of all is lighting the Friday night candles. I don't light candles at the traditional time, just at sunset, because often, especially in the winter months, my guests have not yet arrived and I feel it crucial that this act not be a solitary one; rather, I see it as an initiation which creates community out of all of those who will be sharing the evening. I wait till everyone is present and we are ready to sit down to dinner. We gather around the dining room table. The other lighting in the room is soft, dim, though bright enough to see the familiar faces of family and old friends, and the new faces of people I'm only just coming to know but have sensed for whatever intangible reason belong at the Friday night table. I light the candles, I cover my eyes, and there in the quiet darkness I enter a world where blessings are available, where blessings flow, and one by one I call up the faces of those people who are most precious to me and the faces of those whose silent presence surrounds me in the darkened room. I allow blessing to flow through me and to wash over each beloved soul in turn. Finally, I invoke the power of blessing on my own behalf, then I chant the Hebrew words which sanctify the fire of the candles and I open my eyes to enter the spirit home I have labored to create.

This is the home, week after week, year after year, into which I welcomed our Hillel students. It was with them that I developed Friday night as a spiritual art form. Many of them knew from birth the rituals they shared at my Shabbos table, many of them were, as I had been at their age, strangers in a strange land. These few hours each Friday night formed an unacknowledged center in my life. Throughout the '70s, the '80s, into the '90s, when people would ask me, "What do you do?", that thorny old question which through the years has plagued women and probably many men as well, that question which is really asking "Who are you?" but setting the narrowest parameters for response, when people would ask me, "What do you do?" I would answer always with what my paid employment was at the time, as if what

I was paid to do was the only real way of defining myself. (A favorite "click" moment of mine, à la *Ms.* magazine, came many years ago when filling out forms for a driver's license: I wrote for *occupation* "teacher/writer," then for *employer* I wrote "unemployed." The clerk transferring my written form to his computer digested my words and without even looking up at me typed in simply "housewife.") In fact though, it was only after I'd won my first playwriting grant—again, the crucial factor, the pivotal factor, being money—it was only then I felt when asked "What do you do?"—I was entitled to respond "I'm a playwright." But in all my years, never, never would I have dreamt of identifying myself by saying, "I make Shabbos." Even though through all the changes of my identity and the realities of my worldly life, that is perhaps the single activity which has most consistently and profoundly defined meaning for me. Maybe only as you are marching toward fifty do you begin to envision approaching your life with that kind of courage.

But I've left you standing at the Shabbos table. The candles are lit, we all move about the room, hugging, kissing, wishing each other Good Shabbos, Good Shabbos. Now we sit, we hold hands round the table, families, strangers, old and young, men and women, girls and boys, together we sing or hum along in harmony traditional songs to welcome the Sabbath. Eddie praises me with "Eshet Chayil," the psalm which enumerates the qualities of the good woman, I parallel his appreciation by singing "Mi HaIsh" to him; together we embrace our children and invoke upon them the ancient priestly blessing: "May God bless you and watch over you, May God's face shine upon you with kindness, May God's face be lifted toward you granting you peace." Eddie makes kiddush over the wine, I uncover the braided challahs and hold them aloft as I bless them as well. Whoever judges himself least tired from the week gets up to serve the soup.

# 3

*The Necessity of Poetry in My Life*

Many words were required to adequately describe the journey I took from a secular childhood in Brooklyn, a childhood perhaps best described as religiously two-dimensional, to the richness, depth, fullness of an adult spirituality. Fewer words are needed to explain the necessity of poetry in my life.

I began to write poetry in the early 1980's when, already in my thirties, I participated in a week-long workshop on Jewish feminism led by Judith Plaskow and Rabbi Ruth Sohn at an adult learning seminar, the National Havurah Summer Institute. From the very first session of the workshop, we noted that there was little that Jewish women could turn to when celebrating lifecycle events and so some of us in that course gave ourselves nightly homework assignments to begin to fill the void we experienced in Jewish liturgy and literature.

A case in point: while the tradition offers prayers and blessings for an extraordinary range of life experiences—everything from acknowledging the presence of a rainbow in the sky, to drawing attention to the small daily miracle of the body ridding itself of poisonous waste after a night's sleep—there was no prayer to be found that a woman could say after suffering a miscarriage. My first homework assignment for that Jewish feminist workshop, an assignment I gave myself really, was to write something—a prayer, a poem, a meditation—marking the occasion of a miscarriage.

I didn't know what to say, I didn't know how to begin. First was the problem of my lack of confidence with the form. As a child I wrote poetry all the time—I could barely make it home the three blocks from school most days without a poem forming in my mind and demanding to be recorded immediately; the problem then was only to find a scrap of paper on which to write. So I would have to say that poetry was at first a natural act for me, like eating, laughing, skipping.

In college I took an introductory creative writing course. The teacher had us write a one-act play, a few short stories, and a portfolio of poetry. Classtime was taken up with his reading aloud whichever student work he assessed as being most promising. I don't recall his ever reading my work. For the most part he read the work of male students. (This was a time in my life before I understood what a misogynist was.) I still remember my one-act play—I think it was quite good; the short stories I remember not at all. But most clearly, I remember when I got back my portfolio of poems. He had written nothing on the individual poems themselves—no marginal comments, no end comments, no corrections, no observations. Just three words scrawled on the cover of the portfolio: "Stick to prose." For the next fifteen years one of the things I knew about myself was that I could not write poetry.

A second problem as I faced the blank page that late afternoon in August 1983, trying to do my homework for the Jewish feminist workshop: if this was a prayer, presumably it was "addressed" to God and so should begin with some sort of salutation, otherwise it would be rude. But how should I address God? What did I believe about God, what actually could I call God? And sitting there at the community pool, bathed in late afternoon sunlight, surrounded by the laughter and splashing and chaos of many children, including my four year old Lisa and one year old Uri, a life so full of blessing, even at that moment, as I called up the memory of my miscarriage seven years before, I had nothing nice to say to God.

I decided to skip the salutation. Eddie watched the kids while I went off to an outlying picnic table and wrote—a prayer? a poem?—honest words about a time long ago when my heart broke. I cried and I wrote, I wrote and I cried, I went to class the next day and read what I'd written and my teachers and fellow students cried. And then we told each other our stories about miscarriage, our stories about the times our bodies had betrayed us, our stories about the times we learned to hate and fear God.

I discovered that week that writing poetry offered me a way of integrating the seemingly disparate spheres of my life— seeker, feminist, Jew, mother, writer, daughter, wife, woman. Writing poetry also gave me a way, in fact many ways, of talking to God, something I didn't think of myself as having done easily before that time.

Over the years my explorations as a Jewish feminist and as a spiritual seeker have taken me down many roads. Some of the time I've walked the road with others, working to establish Jewish community—a particular group of people in a particular time and place who've decided to trust one another, to violate polite distance just enough to warm each other a little.

At other times my search has taken me down solitary roads. Alone in my study, I've written plays that explore the Yom Kippur liturgy and our yearning for wholeness, for reconciliation. I've interpreted biblical tales and biblical folk, as well as the tests we moderns face when God calls out our name and we must respond "hineni"—here I am.

And then there was the time I made my home in Jerusalem, bought my fruit in the shuk, sent my children off to Israeli schools, reached out to strangers, especially women, working for peace.

In the following pages, some of the paths I want to share with you are the ones I've travelled as a poet, a Jewish feminist poet.

The poet, as she journeys, is like a human camera. She takes in the details—the smell of the Shabbos cholent, the glistening sweat after the wedding dance, the sound of the dirt as it hits the coffin. All the details are collected, stored away by the poet. And then she sits, with pen, with paper, and makes a record, a particular picture, along the road we travel.

In some of my poems, attention is drawn to empty spaces, to silences that were crying out all this time, to characters who seemed invisible though they stood right before us. Sometimes attention is drawn to the absence of God. These poems may be wistful, or angry, or anguished. Alternately, other poems capture moments in which God—that spirit which sustains us, which nourishes us—seems present in the world, at least in the frame of the picture, and that presence is celebrated.

Many of my poems are prayers—not in any conventional sense, but rather in the most primal sense.

What is a prayer? A prayer is the articulation of something very particular at the core of one's being, flung out into the universe. Perhaps it finds a mark, perhaps not. The essential thing is the articulation and the flinging.

# 4

*Report from the Trenches*

With a hubris perhaps more characteristic of baby boomers than those of earlier or later generations, I assumed when I finally decided to take the leap of faith that had been urged upon me—to have a child—that I'd get pregnant right away and deliver a perfect baby nine months later. But that wasn't meant to be my story. I took a leap of faith, the ground I landed on didn't hold.

The poemprayer with which I open this volume, "Healing after a miscarriage," is a response to the unnatural—you conceive a child, the child is supposed to burrow in, be at home, grow. That didn't happen. Perhaps the tradition had wisdom to offer here, wisdom for women (and men) who felt this pain of loss, this betrayal of their own bodies, but such old wisdom has been lost to us. When I wrote "Healing" in the early '80s, I knew of no other such words. Now there is a growing record of women sharing these experiences and feelings, also a growing wisdom which recognizes the need to acknowledge loss, the need for ritual, the need to grieve.

Twenty years after my miscarriage, a couple who were congregants of Eddie's miscarried twins and asked him to officiate at the funeral. When it was over, he and I began walking home together, hand in hand. After a few wordless blocks I began to cry, stopped walking, and there on Amsterdam Avenue we stood holding each other amidst the Upper West Side bustle of noonday shoppers and food deliveries. "It's not that I would have wanted to do a funeral," I said, "but we had no ritual to help us at all." "We never really marked the moment," I sobbed. And then the realization, simultaneous to us both— I guess what I did, all those years after, was to write the poem . . .

# Healing after a miscarriage

Nothing helps. I taste ashes
in my mouth. My eyes are flat,
dead. I want no platitudes,
no stupid shallow comfort.
I hate all pregnant women,
all new mothers, all soft babies.

The space I'd made inside myself
where I'd moved over
to give my beloved room to grow—
now there's a tight angry
bitter knot of hatred there instead.

What is my supplication?
Stupid people and new mothers,
leave me alone.
Deliver me, Lord,
of this bitter afterbirth.
Open my heart
to my husband-lover-friend
that we may comfort each other.
Open my womb
that it may yet bear
living fruit.

What comes next? For me what came next was the gift of children. When I began to write poetry, I was the mother of babies, of toddlers. I wrote out of a spiritual need to articulate my reality, to give voice to the layers of truth I found myself uncovering as the adventure of living with children unfolded.

I don't see it as coincidental that I began writing in earnest after I became a mother. For me, deciding to allow children into my life, "moving over to give them room to grow," was an opening to creativity on many levels. Children insist that you give your all. And then they demand that you give more. They demand that you give what you didn't know you had to give. And part of what they give back is the chance to know much better who you are and what you're capable of.

# Birthing Blessings

I am so thankful on this day for strength
of spirit and body to endure pain, to be
courageous, for a baby, alive and healthy.

I have wondered for so long what you would
look like—wondrous eyes? dimpled chin?
swarthy? ruddy? all the fingers? all the toes?

And today I am touching you, touching you,
caressing you, possessing you, blessing you,
with my fingers, my eyes, lips, heavy breasts.

We are more one than ever, little bird.
Who are you, little bird—are you a bird?
perhaps a lion dwells within? a bear cub?

a pussycat? maybe a gazelle. Who knows—
you will tease out from me in time
all such love names and many more, many more.

I evoke the spirit of my mother, my mother's
mother, all the fierce soft loving mothers
down the ages—help me to find within

the strength I possess, the warm nourishing
milk, the kisses, tenderness, caresses,
the discipline, wisdom, self-control.

Help me to gather all my womanly forces
to mother this baby, to protect and nurture
and guide this new, yet undiscovered soul.

And let me not curse the child
or myself when we both prove
to be only human.

The haze of those early newborn days . . . the ecstasy of holding, touching, kissing . . . the mind-numbing blur of exhaustion . . . the terror of total and permanent responsibility. I remember how for the first few weeks I was afraid to be left alone in the house with "her." We lived right off campus; a student came a few hours a day to help with the laundry, to straighten up the kitchen. At least that's what I told her I was paying her for. Her real function was simply to be a physical presence in the house, to somehow shore up my courage in learning to care for a totally helpless creature who might at any moment demand something vital I would prove too incompetent to provide . . . How long did it take until I felt at ease being alone with my own baby? A long time . . .

Slowly they grow, you learn, they help you to relax, to forget your fear. Eventually you see that you're going to be OK. Life settles into a routine. If you're lucky, your baby naps.

# The Nap

*Do you flush? When she's napping—*
*Do you flush?*
*No,* I say to the voice on the other end of the phone.
We both laugh.
Another mother's secret shared.

When I put her down
I take the phone off the hook,
wrap the receiver in a dish towel,
and then stick it in my purse.
I take off my shoes
and tiptoe around in my socks,
gathering books, magazines, sections of the newspaper,
something to nosh, pen, writing paper,
my latest quilting project—
enough to sustain me for days, weeks.
I tiptoe it all into the living room
and then I sit.

Sometimes I ignore it all,
immediately asleep myself.
Or I stare out the window,
let my mind wander,
accountable to no one.

Most often, with exquisite luxury,
I choose a book, the sewing, perhaps Sunday's magazine section.
And of course I only risk going to the bathroom—
and passing her door—
if my bladder is so full I can't concentrate any more.

But then the neighbor's dogs go crazy,
or the parcel postman rings the bell

(it's never for me, always for
one of the women on the block
who works all day)
and then I hear her.
The break is over
I'm a mother again.

Up the stairs
open the door
I fling my arms out wide
and we embrace like sentimental old Italians.
I kiss all the flesh I can get my mouth to—
her neck
her cheeks
her nose
her eyes
I babble love nonsense to her
and she in turn strokes my face.

I thought those days would never end.

The central ritual the tradition provides for new life is for new sons—the bris. Circumcision represents entrance into the covenant with God. As it happened, our firstborn was a girl. We planned a naming ceremony for her, still a novelty in 1978, which included a reading from the Torah, the joyous singing of Hallel, words about who she was named for, room for guests to offer her their blessings. And of course, food. Then when our son was born, we naturally just adapted the naming ceremony we'd previously devised. It had only one essential difference from our daughter's celebration.

# My Friends Baked Cake and We Ordered Lox and Whitefish from the Deli

I stood there shoulder to shoulder with the men
when they hacked a piece off your little thing—
could I really sit in the room next door
and let my fantasies run wild when I heard you cry?

And yet, at the crucial moment, I wasn't watching.
I was staring off into space at some invisible focal point.
The same one I'd stared at through the hours of labor?
Maybe.
Maybe the same one Sarah stared at
when Abraham took her baby up to the mountain.

I'm not angry, but you know,
you're a little weird, you male Jewish God.
What do you need with all those foreskins anyway?

So many pictures we could take of family life, of the same family, and all would be true and all would be different: here we are, see us, we are cuddling at bedtime, we are reading a story. And here we are, just in from sledding and we're making hot chocolate. And here we are, bathed, fresh clothing, glowing faces gathered around the Shabbos table.

The picture of "The Nap" reflects a truth most young parents recognize, but it is not the only truth. There are other truths, darker truths, the kind it's hard to talk about. You look around at the other mothers you know, you wonder, "Does she lose her patience as often as I do? Does she want to escape as desperately as I do? Is she someone I could confide in, trust?"

Once, before I myself was a mother, I remember a friend telling me the following story: In the early '60s, she lived in a Manhattan apartment building, one with a pocket park across the street. Each morning the mothers, babies, and toddlers would pour out of the building and congregate in the park. For the children it was a chance to soak up some sunshine, get a workout on the playground equipment, parallel play with the other youngsters. For the mothers of course it was a lifeline to companionship, advice, adult conversation. One fall morning the mothers congregated to chat and noticed that Cynthia was there without her two year old. "Where's Jeffrey?" her friends inquired. "He's up in his room," was the response. The other women were incredulous—"Is he safe up there alone?" "For the moment, he's safer up there alone than if I were with him," replied Cynthia.

Over the years when my children were little and went through periods when they would test me, push me, periods when I struggled to maintain my equilibrium, I would call to mind this story, I would buy a little extra babysitter time, ask a friend to spell me for an hour or two. Go for a walk, take myself to the movies, have a hot fudge sundae.

# Report from the trenches

I stopped nursing this morning.
Actually, I'm not yet sure I've stopped.
Let's just say this morning I didn't nurse.
It's almost 17 months.

I have so little to give him.
I feel I'm in a desert
and have so little to give him.
I need to do for me,
to nurse myself.

I'm very angry
at his tremendous power
at my loss of control.
I just want to be left alone
to have my body to myself again
to center myself again.

Won't someone help me?
I don't know how to make it clear
that I'm in trouble.
(I feel like I'm always in trouble—
the mother who cried wolf?)
Every day I work so hard
not to hit him.
Sometimes, overcome by rage,
I shake him.
How do you think I feel about myself
when I do that?

Once, many years ago,
I saw a friend hit her 7 year old for talking fresh,
her 2 year old for spilling some chocolate milk.
I was shocked at how strict she was.

I had no idea that wasn't the point at all.
The point was, she was right on the edge,
about to go over,
calling for help.
(She did in fact go over.)

Couldn't somebody maybe help me?
If I pulled my pockets inside out
to show how empty I am
would that get through to you?

The trouble is
there are three kinds of people—
the ones who've never been there
and so don't understand,
the ones who are there now
and can barely stay afloat themselves,
and the ones who've got it all behind them
and wouldn't go back for all the world.

Thank God for babysitters and grandmothers,
although not everyone can afford them.

Looking back on those years, the years of caring for toddlers and young children especially, I see now that I didn't get enough help for myself. I was ashamed to feel overburdened by the demands of being the stay-at-home Mom. Our culture so devalues and disrespects those who devote themselves to caring for young children that to feel you are failing as a fulltime mother triggers an almost bottomless loss of self-respect, increasing the possibility for losing control, for lashing out in anger and violence. Ironically, just when your resources are most depleted, you need to marshall the strength and courage to say, "I need help, I need support," to say it clearly and loudly enough to be heard. It's vital to do so—call out to friends, to members of your extended family, to professionals: I need help. It doesn't signal failure or shame, it signals that you are doing the most important work of all, need and deserve support and assistance to do it well and wisely, like all the mothers who've come before you.

And we who are not in the midst of tending little ones ourselves need to be attentive and full-of-care to those who are, we need to check in on them, keep track of how they are doing, listen carefully and support them through hard times. Precious gifts: kind, sympathetic, respectful listening that allows a young mother to unburden her heart; a few hours of filling in so she can be alone with her own thoughts, dreams, breathing.

Despair, bliss, despair, bliss. And it's only Tuesday. It's only 11 in the morning. Despair again. Bliss again.

## two

the smell of your hair
is making me crazy
with pleasure

for months, we've been at odds
you, fanning my anger
calculating where my limit is
then pushing me beyond it

me, overwhelming you with rage
terrorizing you with a look
an ungentle touch

and now
at last
some peace
released into love
quiet passion

we flirt
we linger
over every touch

I can't get enough
of the smell of your hair

Most especially when our children are little we are prime mediators between them and the world. Consciously and unconsciously, we give them myriad signals all day long: now is the time to listen; it's good to smile at people; it's OK to get your clothes dirty when you play; you can't take cookies from the serving plate and put them back on the serving plate; do not hit when someone takes your toy—use words. Every moment we are bombarded by choices, and make twenty more without even thinking about them—what do I teach this child about appropriate behavior, socially acceptable behavior, what are my values and how do I help this little person strike a balance between expressing her unique self versus learning to function in society. It is my job as a parent to do both, but mostly these two functions are at odds. Every day, every moment, we are making choices as parents.

# Ritual of Brushing the Hair

*Ow!* she screams
*You're pulling my sculp!*

I love those words
I don't correct her
I never correct those words.

I leave it to others
to make those corrections.

I say
*I'm sorry*
*I'll try to be gentle.*

Many years ago some close friends who had struggled long and hard to become parents succeeded: they adopted a child. As they prepared to bring her home, the father told of tying a little red ribbon to the corner of the crib. My friend the rationalist, the prominent intellectual, explained that it was an old superstition: keeping a bit of red fabric with the baby served as protection. "Why not?" he said.

Red ribbons were not my personal favorite. I found my own superstitious expressions. My friend Aaron, whose pleasure it was to work with wood, made me a palm-sized block combining black walnut, oak, and pine. He claimed since I seemed incapable of expressing any good tidings whatsoever (most especially regarding my children) without the primitive response of "knocking wood," he wanted to provide me with a portable piece of it to be sure I always felt prepared to ward off the evil eye.

There's more at stake here than red ribbons and wood though. Every time I say "knock wood" to my friend Veronika— "Lisa is flourishing this year, knock wood"—she liturgically corrects me with, "Thank God." Veronika is trying to make a point, she's asserting something, I know. She is trying to get me to see something, to acknowledge something—blessings are not random, blessings flow from God.

There are moments in my life when I have experienced that as a visceral truth; but in other moments I feel betrayed, I have lost my faith, my ability to trust. I am angry, I am separate, I do not feel myself to be a part of the divine flow. It is at times a source of great conflict: I want to protect those who are most precious to me, but where and to whom can I turn for help?

Whether we try to assert some modicum of control with a red ribbon, by knocking wood, or by invoking the Source of Divinity, there is absolutely no question that our children make us hostages to fate.

# Croup

*Croup is a children's respiratory ailment—*
*suddenly a child can't breathe. Moist air may*
*relieve the condition, if not, emergency hospital-*
*ization is necessary. Sometimes croup is fatal.*

At night
in our bed,
rigid,
listening,
listening for that breathing.

And then
racing to the bathroom,
hot water,
steam.

We take turns holding him—
thirty pounds, fighting for air—
together we hold him
(how does a single parent do this?)
the steam condensing on the three of us.
I've never loved you more
than this moment
in our bathroom.

I don't let him feel my fear,
I take all of his fear into me
and finally, the heavy little body relaxes
back into his crib.

I love you so much,
I love you so much.

And you God—I hate you—
I hate you with all my heart,
with my clenched teeth,
with my clenched fists,
with my fingernails I hate you
for playing with me and my little boy.

And you God—thank you,
thank you—I kiss your feet—
You let me keep my little boy.
I'll be so good
You won't be sorry.

My friend Kathy's parents fled Hitler in the 1930s and emigrated to Levenworth, Kansas where Kathy was born and grew up. She used to relay her parents' perrenial observation when she was a child in Levenworth: "We seem to need to pack more supplies in the car to go for a day's outing to Kansas City than we took with us leaving Germany."

That is the nature of a household with children—the sheer amount of equipment these small people require to get through a day is astounding. And even if you as a parent determine not to become overwhelmed by material goods, even if you consciously fight the American acquisitive malaise, you will still probably need to purchase for your baby a crib, a stroller, a highchair.

I don't have what I would consider to be a mature or healthy relationship to money. Because I grew up poor, and because I was a child of the '60s, I had a two-fold reason to scorn the acquisition of things. My particular working out of the dysfunction with which I grew up has been to make money when I can and to spend as little of it as I can. For most of my adult life I've lacked the confidence to spend money, I feel safer being parsimonious. I've never wanted to have a long way to fall. It's a decades-old comedy routine in our marriage that Eddie, who like many men, enjoys toys, would say, "Let's get a Cuisinart . . . let's get a computer . . . let's get a VCR . . . " and I'd respond, "We don't need that—people have gotten along just fine without that . . . " (Eventually he'd entice me to join him on a shopping expedition and then I'd become a devotee of the latest technological luxury.)

Beautiful things are a separate category—when I would see a stunning piece of pottery or a wooden salad bowl exquisitely wrought, I would alleviate my consumer guilt by purchasing the object as a gift for a friend. Only recently have I allowed myself to sometimes make purchases when the item in question was beautiful and to keep it for my own pleasure, to, in effect, buy myself a gift. This small step in maturity I credit in part to the purchase of a highchair.

# Highchair

We didn't buy the oak highchair,
the handsome one we liked—
it seemed impractical,
hard to clean.

We bought the chrome instead:
foam padded seat and back,
textured plastic with green and
yellow elephants and giraffes.

Feeding them was fun at first,
mashed banana and familia.
Then fun became habit,
cottage cheese and yogurt.
Finally familiarity breeds contempt—
"Don't throw your eggs on the floor!"

Six years, two children later,
without sentiment
I put it at the curb on trash day,
disgusting, torn beyond repair,
unfit to hand down to a friend.

Hardly a day had gone by
when I hadn't thought,
we should have bought
the handsome oak one.

Babies outgrow their highchairs. They grow and grow and suddenly you don't have babies anymore. Those toddlers, those kindergarteners, those 8 year olds who still clamber into your bed on snowy mornings, creating exotic tents with your comforter, ready to travel to imaginary kingdoms—they were here, right here, now they're gone.

Alison Lurie in *The War Between the Tates* captured one aspect of this memorably for me, as the mother in the novel reflects:

> They were a happy family once. Jeffrey and Matilda were beautiful, healthy babies; charming toddlers; intelligent, lively, affectionate children . . . Then last year, when Jeffrey turned fourteen and Matilda twelve, they had begun to change; to grow rude, coarse, selfish, insolent, nasty, brutish and tall. It was as if she were keeping a boarding house in a bad dream, and the children she had loved were turning into awful lodgers—lodgers who paid no rent, whose leases could not be terminated.

# Yom Kippur Break

Twenty years ago
I sat with a friend
under a magnolia tree,
we sat on the ground
during the break
on Yom Kippur
and she poured out her heart to me.

She was older than I,
she had children,
and that was what we talked about.

She loved the daughter fiercely
and was afraid of her:
*When the adolescent tempest*
*is howling and roaring*
*going full pitch*
*she'll break me.*

*She'll do with closed door*
*turned back, curled lip*
*what drunken father, dead mother*
*indifferent lover, serpentine colleague*
*never could do—*
*she'll break me.*

Newly married, just having started
looking my own mother in the eye again,
I replied, *No, no*
*you reap what you sow,*
*I'm sure of it.*

My daughter is twelve now,
I know I should be guarded,

develop strategies
for collateral attachments,
wean myself from kisses,
from her gentle admiration,
probably I'm riding for a fall.
But I now confirm
what I've always secretly known—
I'm reckless at love.

Maybe she'll break me.

Both my children were born in Princeton and in many ways lived out a childhood I had only dreamed of: a little house on a tree-lined street, each with a room of their own, a huge unfinished attic big enough both for storage of exotic old family junk and corners to hide in for pretend games on rainy afternoons. When my friend Aaron the carpenter agreed to make Lisa a dollhouse for her third birthday, it was on one condition: "Recognize, Merle, that it's really for you. Train sets and dollhouses are about the child who lives inside the parent."

I wanted so much for Lisa's childhood to be safe, to be happy, to have none of the pain that had been my growing up companion. (I never really worried for Uri's happiness—I reasoned from the example of my brothers that boys were sturdy and naturally happy. By now I look back and realize it's not that boys were sturdy and naturally happy but rather they were not given the option of having feelings. They learned stickball instead.)

I was vigilant with Lisa as I suspect many mothers are with their daughters. I thought my role as the good mother was to be on guard constantly not only against germs and traffic and suspicious looking strangers, but most of all against the cruelty of peers and playmates.

How many of us understand until the opportunity is long gone that we serve our children best by letting them fall and bruise and see, yes, they are sturdy, fall again in a new way and learn and heal and grow. That they need us not as bodyguards but as teachers, as appreciative audiences, as advisors, as companions who model being joyous in the world.

As we prepared to move from Princeton, leaving the attic and the days of childhood behind, I found myself reflecting on the passing of a part of my own life as mother to a little girl.

# I was watching

I have spent half a lifetime
sitting in this chair
looking out this window
watching to see
if anyone was being mean
to you. I never thought
to sit in this chair
and look out this window
just for the pleasure
of observing you at play.

And now you are a tall girl
with a woman's body,
too old to play in public.
And now the moment to watch
for pleasure is gone.
And I grieve that for all
the watching I never caught
you in a single moment
of simple childish pleasure,
not that I can recall.

Now Lisa is a young adult and when she comes home for a weekend visit, as I listen to the tales of her adventures, I experience a joy being in her presence I was unable to allow myself in the early years when I was singlemindedly intent on vigilance, when I felt personally responsible for every tear.

Norman Frimer, may his memory be for a blessing, was right all those many years ago when he advised me in my particular struggle for faith to climb over my doubts and my fears to finally have a child: how I have learned and grown through being a mother. Now that they are past adolescence, I finally feel just about prepared to shephard toddlers! But life doesn't work that way. Thankfully my children have generous natures and seem willing to forgive many mistakes and much ineptitude on my part, understanding how earnestly I have tried and how deeply I love them.

# 5

*Passion*

So many kinds of love. When we are courageous we enter each day, each relationship, seeing within it the possibilities for arousal, for devotion, for feelings powerful enough to overwhelm.

What a dangerous way to live, to live as a lover. So we learn to be wise, with our feelings, with our fingers, we learn to be careful. Women especially are taught to be careful, are urged to be careful.

What have I wanted to teach my daughter, my son, about love? And what have I already taught in a thousand ways when I was just living, living my ordinary day-to-day life, unaware how my every move was being recorded, catalogued, deconstructed. What did I learn growing up in my own childhood home?

*I knew my mother loved my father because she never challenged him, never confronted him. She treated him respectfully. It was her way.*

*I knew my father loved my mother because on an ordinary Saturday morning, if a Cole Porter song came on the radio, he would put his newspaper down, take the dustcloth from her hand, and there in the living room with the morning sunlight streaming through the windows, he'd dance with her. It was his way.*

And what is my way? I have many ways—of showing love, of feeling love, of expressing love. Many ways of taking it in, many ways of shutting it out, many openings to arousal.

# The first time we made Shabbos together

The first time we made Shabbos together
in our own home—
it wasn't really "our home"
it was your third floor walk-up
and we weren't even engaged yet—
I had cooked chicken,
my first chicken,
with a whole bulb of garlic—
my mother never used garlic—
and we sat down at that second-hand chrome table
in the kitchen.
It was all so ugly that we turned out the lights.
Only the Shabbos candles flickered.

And then you made kiddush.

I sat there and wept—
Oh God, you have been so good to me!
Finally, for the first time in my life,
you gave me something I wanted.
This man, whose soul is the soul of Ein Gedi.
We will be silent together,
we will open our flowers in each other's presence.

And indeed we have bloomed through the years.

When we say to children, to teenagers, you want to be sure you share important common commitments and values with a future mate, we are saying something much deeper than a young person can perhaps appreciate. (I remember thinking when my mother said that to me—"How boring that sounds!") What we as parents are trying to express is the deep kinship of soul that is needed to nourish a couple through all the difficult and challenging twists and turns life can present.

When Lisa was 3 or 4 years old, her best friend was Peter, a neighbor on the block whose parents were Christian. One day Lisa confided in me, "When I grow up, I want to marry Peter." My first reaction was, she's so little, there's no point in making something of this; but then I thought, best to provide a reality check. I said, "Peter is a wonderful boy and a wonderful friend, but Peter is not Jewish—how will you have Friday night if you marry Peter?" Lisa, who cherished our Friday nights more than anything, seemed to respond to the simple logic of that analysis.

When Uri was 12 or 13 and we were by that time living on the Upper West Side, he engaged me in conversation one day about intermarriage. He made an excellent case for the value of all peoples and the possibility that he as a Jew could come to love someone who was not Jewish. Oh, I thought, I have a great response, remembering back to 4-year-old Lisa. "But if you married someone who wasn't Jewish, how would you have Friday night?" I asked. Uri, who had quickly grown accustomed to the many sophisticated delights of New York City, looked at me with that calm and patient look he gets when, say, he's listening to me talk through a problem I'm having—I'm agitated, emotional, but he's easy, calm. He's got a gift for that special kind of patience. How would he have Friday night with a non-Jewish partner? His unruffled response: "Take out."

I was 21 when I married Eddie. I had lived virtually all my life in the same twenty block radius in Brooklyn, and suddenly I was moving a thousand miles away, leaving behind everyone else I had ever loved or known to make a home with a man it seemed like I had just met. How do you come to decide to commit yourself to spending the rest of your life with a particular person? I thought a lot about that, then and since, felt profoundly challenged by the utter irrationaiity of that.

# Logic

Because you were handsome in a black turtleneck
and leaned over your Talmud in an inviting way,
I took a chance and married you.

Now suddenly
by the front door
a yellow bike with training wheels,
three broken strollers
growing mold in the basement,
pencil scribbles on the walls upstairs,
fights about money.

A leap of faith.
A marriage.

As we were preparing for our wedding, a friend and rabbinic classmate of Eddie's, a novice calligrapher, volunteered to make us a ketubah, a wedding contract. Nowadays, as in older times and other cultures, calligraphy, watercolor, papercuts have all come into vogue again as couples commission artists to create their ketubot, but then it was new, different. Now in fact artists consult with bride and groom about themes to incorporate into the text, designs and symbols with special meaning for the couple. Our calligrapher was just starting out though—all he wanted was our Hebrew names. It was then that I realized I didn't have one, or more precisely, no one in the family could remember what it was. So I got to choose a name. "*Malka Aliza*" sounded like "Merle Lizbeth" and I liked the meaning: joyous queen.

Then years later when our first child was born and we were again thinking about names, Eddie wanted to choose a new name for himself, for the new person he was becoming: a father. "*Ephraim*" was the name his parents had given him, he now prefaced that with "*Adam*" (in Hebrew, pronounced a-DAMM)—first person, first man, new man.

It's a powerful feeling when you are moving through some important life passage—becoming part of a committed couple, becoming a parent—on some level you are becoming a new person, all of what you have been is realigning and being born anew.

# On Our Fifteenth Anniversary

*At a traditional Jewish wedding the guests dance while carrying the bride and groom aloft on chairs as if they were a king and queen.*

I know you didn't want to wear a rented tux,
and you didn't want a bourgeois Brooklyn wedding,
and you thought my hair looked ridiculous
(I haven't been in a beauty parlor since).

But it was a golden day,
a forever shining day,
when they lifted us on chairs—
a King and Queen.

We danced, we danced,
my heart is breaking,
I feel so blessed
*Adam Ephraim.*

Love is a dance, we move back and forth. Sometimes we are so close it is impossible to tell where I leave off and you begin. I touch you and the pleasure of it fills me, but isn't touching you about how I give you pleasure, not about how I am pleasured? The answer is, it is all one flow of pleasure, the touching and the being touched. I am aching with pleasure, with the giving and the receiving of pleasure, aching with the confusion of pleasure.

Other times we stand as if on two opposite shores, the roar of the water separating us makes it hard to hear—are you speaking the language of intimacy which we share, or some strange new incomprehensible tongue? And what are those gestures you're making—I can't see well, I can't interprete accurately.

Sometimes when we are far away from someone beloved we talk on the phone and the distance melts, our souls mingle, we close our eyes and the voice is lying beside us as it always does. But other times, the barriers are rigid, they remain intact. You realize he is someplace where he cannot be fully himself, he can't give himself to you in the accustomed ways. You put down the phone at the end of the conversation and feel lonelier than before.

# A Bad Connection

In your parents' apartment
there is one phone
on a short cord
in the kitchen.

Across the many miles
as you hold the phone
in that tiny apartment

where the water dripping
in the bathroom sink
hears the breathing of the one
who lies in the bedroom
hears the chewing of a candy
in a living room chair

in that tiny apartment
you cannot bring yourself
to say to me
I miss you
I love you
your new book is beautiful
I ache to touch your face
your breasts.

In your parents' apartment
you are on a short cord.

How rare, when the love between two people is easy, when it opens like a flower and you say what you feel and the words are heard the way you thought you said them. I remember thinking, when I was in high school, when I was in college, that my awkwardness was somehow a part of this adolescent/young adult stage of life. I thought, when I'm an adult, fully a woman, I'll be graceful in expressing love, in making connection. But the truth is, all too often, criticism, rebuke, angry words jump out of us unbidden. The truth is, misunderstanding is the norm: it's always hard to express love.

What are we afraid of? We are afraid of making ourselves vulnerable, we are afraid of being in pain. We are afraid of looking foolish. We are afraid of unleashing powerful emotions, we are afraid that in opening a door, crossing a threshold, we will open a neediness that has no bottom. We are afraid of being misunderstood, we are afraid of being rejected.

The truth is, it's always hard to make connections, not just when we're young and inexperienced but for the whole of our lives it demands a leap of faith and great courage.

# Your soul and my soul

How often do you sit
with someone you love
in the next room
in the next chair

and what is it
that prevents your soul
from leaping up
leaping up to say

*Your soul and my soul,*
*aren't they one?*
*aren't we one?*
*that's how I feel.*

What is it that prevents you?

Instead you sit
in your own room
in your own chair
filled with longing and loneliness

and the moment passes.

At heart I'm a shy person and so I have a particular abhorance for cocktail parties, large receptions, formal dinners: I simply see no point to them. I find it a terrible strain to be expected to make scintillating conversation for an evening with people I've never met before and likely will never see again. I don't want to be bothered to entertain some strange man or woman with clever remarks about the latest Washington debacle, the newest novel reviewed in the *Times,* the state of the contemporary American theatre. And I don't care to spend an evening forced to listen and pretending to care when others ramble on about such matters. I suppose the fundamental falsity of the situtation is what irks me—it forces us to pretend to be jovial good friends when we don't know each other.

It's a waste of precious time to engage in superficial contact. But if I meet the very same person volunteering to staff our neighborhood homeless shelter, waiting for six hours on line at the Passport Office, studying a biblical text on retreat, visiting a house of mourning, if the opportunity for real meeting is possible, then I am present with a full heart and mind and a conversation may ensue which we both will have reason to remember long after. I have little patience for making conversation, I have a bottomless capacity for making connection.

Of all the things I am passionate about, I am most passionate about friendships. They are my deepest pleasure. I am so devoted to so many friends scattered in so many places that AT&T called *me* to solicit my business for their rock bottom corporate rate!

Once I was having lunch with Sharon and I asked how her daughter was doing her first year away at college. "Good," she replied. "She's someone who needs only one or two friends, but they have to be really close." By comparison, she then said of herself, "I want fifty friends, none of them too close." "And you," she continued as we both convulsed in laughter, "you need fifty friends, all of them very close!"

Sometimes people find my appetite for intimacy irresistable, sometimes they find it a strain.

# I wanted so much to be your friend

I wanted so much to be your friend,
your friend for always,

but I did it all wrong,
I always do.

I thought I could tell you
everything,

that you'd love me more,
that I'd be sure it was me you loved.

I thought when someone really loves you
nothing is too much to share—

I guess I was testing your limits,
I guess I found them.

I miss you,
I wish I had settled for less,

I'm sorry I scared you
with my everything, my too much.


Couldn't we say "take two"
as if we were making a movie?

Couldn't I instruct you
"The jury will disregard that"?

Couldn't I rewind the tape
and press the "erase" button?

Couldn't I interrupt your note taking with
"That last part is off the record"?

Couldn't we agree matter-of-factly
that we've just been rehearsing out of town?

Couldn't you return my phone calls?

One of the deepest, most soul-penetrating ways to fall in love is to work together. To share a task you both understand as holy. To be so busy concentrating on the work that you forget to hold back. You offer your best ideas without ego, you think out loud, you let other lesser matters fall by the wayside. You push yourself beyond tired. You forget to care about being seen in the best light.

With Veronika I spent a year of my life in Israel, organizing dialogue groups, meeting with Israelis and Palestinians, especially women, working toward peace. We talked to people and listened more. We encouraged their talking and their listening. What did we accomplish? Peace talk, more and more peace talk. Where will all the talk end? Perhaps some day with peace.

A note of explanation for what follows: on Friday night you light and then bless the candles to usher in Shabhat. The custom is to first strike a match and kindle the light, then to cover your eyes to be alone with your own private thoughts and prayers, finally to say the traditional formulaic blessing, and then to open your eyes to see the light. It comes to feel as though the light is resulting from the blessing and the prayers, not the mechanical striking of a match. Hence, "I closed my eyes to light the candles..."

# On the other side of the world
*for Veronika*

I closed my eyes
to light the candles
and it was you I saw
on the other side of the world,
you were lighting candles too.

I could see the tracks of the comb
through your wet hair,
the part that shows
under your kerchief.
I saw the blouse you were wearing,
white with blue embroidery.
I saw how it stuck to your back
not quite dry from the shower.

Your hands covered your face
but I could feel the concentration
with which you said your prayer.
I imagined that as you paused
to bless the candles,
you included me as I included you.

I write these words tonight
to reach out to you,
as I reached out to you
when I lit the candles,
as I reach out to you now
in all my best prayers.

When I was in grade school we were regularly required to commit poetry to memory. Once a week we would then stand in front of our classmates and recite.

When we were growing up, the favorite source of poetry both for my brother Roger and myself was a green, hardbound volume we had in the house, one of the few books the family owned aside from my father's law books, titled *Modern American and British Poetry.* I loved that book with such a passion. A passion I never realized Roger shared until after both our parents had died and Roger, Warren, and I were divying up the family assets. Warren, quite a bit older than Roger and me, had his own powerful associations with the scant family memorabilia: this book was not one he coveted. But Roger wanted it badly; he was unrelenting and wound up in possession of the volume of poetry. Whenever I'd visit his house after that, I'd almost always pick up the book, look through it, finger the pages. I even made a halfhearted effort to locate a twin with the help of a rare book dealer. (The effort was halfhearted because I knew even an identical copy wouldn't be a substitute for the real thing.) I calculate Roger had the book for seven years, until he died. Then I took it home with me.

What was so special about this book? When I held it in my hands, when I put it close to my face and smelled it, I could remember the sound of my mother's voice reading those poems aloud to us. The pleasure she took in the rhythm of the words was so evident in her voice, it was contagious. Once you got her started, she would go for a long time, and my mother having pleasure was a pleasure to behold.

Someone once said to me, I think not kindly, that she never saw a person have such pleasure from eating ice cream as I obviously had from eating ice cream—I think she didn't approve of my being a large woman, so she had problems with watching me relish fattening food. When we love someone though, it is a deep particular joy to watch them having pleasure. Whatever it is that gives them that pleasure. Uninhibited pleasure—that's what my mother had from *Modern American and British Poetry,* and that's why the book remained precious to Roger and to me.

I am passionate about a great many things. Like my mother, I love the feel of the sun on my skin, on my face. I notice the sky, ever changing. Like my father, I enjoy many foods. Like both my parents, I take pleasure in the rhythm of language. Like no one else in my family, I enjoy hugging, holding, kissing, touching, I am physical with the people I love, I give love easily. It is my pleasure to do so. I thank you God that you created me with this capacity for pleasure.

Being really truthful, we could all come up with an utterly unique list of what inflames us: a winning baseball play, a new seed catalogue, a piece of black walnut waiting to be carved, a particular Rembrandt self-portrait, a special city...

# Jerusalem, I write your name

Jerusalem
I write your name
as long ago I wrote the names
of boys who made me flush
with inexplicable pleasure.

I wrote their names
then linked my name to theirs—
Merle Pearce, Merle Spirn—
an old-fashioned Brooklyn way
for a twelve year old girl
to practice intimacy.

In my notebooks
in calligraphies of infinite variety
I wrote Merle Pearce, Merle Spirn
and my breathing became irregular.

As long ago I wrote the names
I write your name
Jerusalem.

I remember a time when I was startled to learn that the modern era is the first experience men and women commonly have had with extended marriages—for much of the last several centuries, a long marriage was considered to be one of fifteen years. Besides divorce as a way of terminating marriage, perhaps the husband was older and died leaving a surviving wife to remarry, or the wife died in childbirth leaving the man to begin again. The point was, if we as moderns feel stressed and challenged trying to make a go of long-term marriages, we are in fact historically doing something relatively new.

What has helped me to remain in the same marriage for so many years? (This is a very sticky subject: It's not that I view longevity in marriage as an end unto itself. I view it as positive for me because it has been positive for me.) What follows here are some observations.

Some of my mother's modelling or outright advice has been an example in the negative (e.g., the basic attitude that you as wife should go 75% of the way to meet your husband and by doing so you'll meet him in the middle) but some of her notions have proved invaluable during the inevitable difficulties (e.g., never go to bed angry, which I modified into, make heroic efforts never to go to bed not speaking). Since she was of a generation of women who didn't believe in fighting with their husbands, she had offered me no model or practice in how to fight in a marriage: I had to invent for myself concepts like "fight clean"—don't say things that are so cruel or demeaning they can't be forgotten when the fight is over.

Another important principle for me has been, keep your eyes on the prize: don't be bamboozled or intimidated by movies, the media, the other couples you know into thinking that other people are having all the fun, that there are a few stellar romances out there but your relationship is probably one of the vast humdrum majority. In fact, in all likelihood, the person you are married to has as rich a capacity for intimacy, tenderness, excitement as any fantasy lover: the adventure you share together over the years is how to unlock ever increasing capacities for intimacy, tenderness, excitement in each other.

Two pieces of great good fortune: We have never lost respect for each other; and, in bad times, when one of us had the marriage as a low priority, the other had the marriage as a high priority, fighting hard to stay together, to keep love alive. Though that seems serendipitous to me, it probably was no accident.

And two not-so-small pieces of advice: As a woman, particularly if you are a mother, you must discipline yourself to sometimes be really self-centered. Life forever forces us to make choices where not everyone can win, so sometimes choose yourself as the winner. Secondly, especially when children are little, make it a priority to spend time alone as a couple.

We test each other, we poke and prod—where are your limits, what are my needs? When do they collide and what do we do then? How many times can we pick up the pieces and still smile, still remember how to love? How many collisions can we recover from? How do we finally learn what we need to know about loving?

Feeling more and more like dinosaurs, some of us who think we're still young are celebrating big anniversaries. (No way around it—25 is a big anniversary, 35 is a big anniversary!) How do you celebrate, mark such a milestone? There's pressure: be romantic, be splashy, be big, be original, be romantic, be romantic, have the time of your life, be romantic.

# Paris, they say, is for lovers

I am not perfect,
the hotel wasn't perfect,
the restaurants weren't perfect,
Versailles wasn't perfect.

The love I feel for you
is more than perfect,
it makes perfect seem
small, unimportant.
I have everything I need
in you.

# 6

## *Yizkor*

One of our most important spiritual tasks is to make peace with where we came from, to learn to see clearly the facts of our childhood, our growing up years. Who were those people we lived with, really? We need to make peace with them, to learn to accommodate, to be able to take what's nourishing from those memories and those relationships and to move on to become a full self.

Much of what I've written about my parents represents a double looking back: written not only long after I had stopped living as a child in their home, but also written after their deaths, after the possibilities of feedback and response were gone.

And yet, these relationships are not over, in fact, they are not even static. I have found through the years that my parents continue to travel with me, even occasionally undergoing change as I change. Remarkably, a parent who was a source of life can, even from beyond the grave, continue to offer life.

# Happy Birthday Merle

October, late afternoon,
soft FM music on the kitchen radio,
feeding the baby supper,
feeling warm, peaceful, complete.
Cards and phone calls,
everyone's checked in—
Happy Birthday Merle!
and yet.

Strange, not to talk
to my mother on my birthday,
she who created all birthdays.
Small, bustling, ruddy,
always running,
I remember her running,

running to buy me a watch
for my sweet sixteen
(after work, after groceries
before laundry)
she tripped and fell
down the stairs to the IRT,
required several stitches
just above her eyebrow.
She bore the scar ever after,
long after the watch
thrilled me, marked time for me,
joined the other broken watches
in my drawer.

Faint surprise
an awareness in my stomach
it's been seven years already.

What would I tell her
if I could?
what she always hoped to hear:
*I'm happy, Ma. Finally.*
*Really happy with my life.*

Once on my birthday
I sent her a dozen roses—
I got the idea from a Dear Abby
but I never told her that—
she was already dying.

And actually,
the last time we talked,
the night she slipped into a coma,
I sat on her bed
and she told me about
the morning I was born:

> *It was such a beautiful autumn day, crisp, clear,*
> *the leaves turning, brisk morning chill.*
> *I called Dr. Rubenstein—he lived across the street—*
> *and I said, 'I'm in labor, I'll be walking over to the*
> *hospital now.' He was so upset. He just wouldn't have*
> *it—he insisted on driving me. I was sorry really.*
> *It was such a beautiful morning, and I love to walk.*

Happy Birthday Merle.

At the beginning of my play, *Across the Jordan*, the protagonist Daphna, a young Israeli lawyer, struggles to find a way to honor the memory of her recently deceased father. He has been the profound influence on her life; theirs was an increasingly stormy, confrontational relationship. The process of argument in which they were engaged was her pathway to full adulthood, to autonomy, to the inner work of establishing her unique identity in the world. Now, with him gone, how can she complete this process? It could be argued that the play is driven by Daphna's desperate need to continue the ideological battles his death seems to have abruptly and prematurely put an end to. In a final monologue, as she ponders what this religiously and politically conservative patriarch would make of her radical life choices, she offers the following assessment:

> *If my father were alive now, I suppose he wouldn't speak to me, but since he is dead, he no longer has the power to turn his back. We argue still, much as before.*

114

# The First Fight

I'm lying in bed on a Sunday morning
reading poetry. Sharon Olds is telling me
about her father, how he failed her; also
about children, living, unborn or expired.

And suddenly I realize, in my friends'
apartment, I'm lying not five blocks
from the park where we sat
and argued in the spring of 1978.

It started like every other scene
with you. We were sitting together
on a park bench and I was trying to
make conversation. Your silence

had taught me it was my job,
my job to make conversation
and the pain of the silence was mine
when I failed to make conversation.

When I failed to make conversation,
my whole body felt the pain of the silence.
I had failed to draw you out—
it was my job to draw you out.

But that spring day I had had it with
working both parts. Maybe because
I was newly pregnant and that would
have meant working three parts.

I asked you, "What was it like when I was born?" and
"What kind of baby was I?" and "Did Mom have a
hard delivery?" I had purposely asked easy questions,
to make it easy for you to talk. I didn't expect more

than a few monosyllables. But you answered,
"I don't remember." Over and over, "I don't
remember." And finally, annoyed, "It's too long ago
Merle." I joked, I said, "I've heard you tell

stories further back than that." And you,
who never noticed anything about me,
noticed I wasn't smiling. I was sitting there
in my maternity clothes, the navy tee shirt

with the discreet logo "En Route" and my mother
was dead and for the first time in my life
I wasn't smiling at you. It's hard to remember
the rest. Maybe I yelled, "You don't remember

because you never cared about me." Maybe I
yelled and turned on my heel and left him there
in the park to fend for himself and maybe
I walked home alone. It's hard to remember.

But I know that something
happened between us that day.
Something changed, something broke.
Finally there was a little space between us.

On the anniversary of a parent's death, it is customary to light a yahrzeit candle, a candle of remembrance, which burns for the night and the day. (These candles are designed in different ways: the ones I use have a premeasured quantity of wax set in a small glass tumbler and actually tend to burn longer than the requisite twenty-four hours.)

Often I have taken the opportunity of my mother's yahrzeit to write a poem for her, and I see through the years two things: how my relationship to this custom has changed, and how my relationship to my mother changes.

In the first years after my mother's death, I met the custom of observing yahrzeit with the anger I felt at having lost her too early in life. Like Becky, a character in my play *The Gates are Closing*, I railed against the bitter irony of what seemed to me a supremely gentle symbol which left no room for my raging loss:

*I lit the yahrzeit candle for you, Ma. In the living room, on the mantle. I knew you'd want it. But it hurts me. There's something mocking—cheerful?—with that flickering little light . . . I should remember—tell the kids—I don't want it. Don't do that on my account . . . No cheerful little light for me when I'm gone . . .*

# The Third of Kislev

Downstairs in the living room
there's a yahrzeit candle burning;
in my chest an ache, a sadness
which has weighted me all day.

I don't want to remember—
a year of mourning
of being dead myself—
that was enough.

To whose advantage
this yearly pilgrimage
back into darkness.

Don't I do her honor
to remember day by day
and speak of her
when I'm sitting in my house
and walking on my way?

Have I forgotten
the embrace of the womb?
the way the light
fell on her hair
when she sat reading?
her insatiable attentiveness
to all my life's minutia?

Who does it serve
that I light that candle
and rekindle such
depths of pain?

All last night
all today and
now tonight again
I have made myself busy
visiting friends
running errands
cleaning the stove
falling asleep early in my bed.

By tomorrow morning
the light in the living room
will have burnt itself out
and I can go back in there
to put on a record
or at least not lower
my eyes as I scurry past
on the way to the kitchen.

I write these words in the middle of my life. I am busy these days dreaming dreams and seeing how many of them I can make come true. Sometimes I focus on the half of the glass that's empty—the successes which have so far eluded me. But I keep working, I keep trying. In some ways I have so much more than I ever dreamed I would Professionally there are poems and plays and essays and talks, not just written, not just sitting in my drawer, but out there in the world, in people's hands, minds, hearts: my words. It's more than I ever dreamed. It's more than I ever dreamed because I never dreamed. I learned firsthand how dangerous, how costly, how destructive dreaming could be. I was taught not to do it.

My father was a man who dreamed many dreams but couldn't seem to make them come true.

# My father in his chair

In the last years
he sorted through
the pictures of a lifetime
carefully selecting those
with the power
to transport him
to better worlds.

With those pictures
he became once more
a traveller.
Sitting in his chair
he'd close his eyes
and disappear
to better worlds.

Lillian, Lillian,
with her
he was 20
in tennis whites
the sun was shining
he moved confidently
toward success.

What picture
will be enough
to say it all for me
when I am alone
in my chair
at the end of time?

I asked a dear friend recently, a man considerably older than I, if he was afraid of death. No, he said, I'm afraid of what comes before . . .

We see first with our parents, then with ourselves, how little by little, aging deprives us of control, of power. Even in our forties, we already see how the body begins to betray us. Part of the hard reality of aging are incremental physical limitations, but what often accompanies those inevitable ravages of time is even more damaging—a shrinking of the spirit. Only some of us seem to be gifted with the wisdom of knowing how to stay attached to life. Full of passion, full of love, like my mother's mother who lived well into her eighties. Perhaps she never lost her self because she was so well practiced in tethering that self to the lives of all around her. It is a gift, a life skill, all too rare.

For many years I was one of the very few amongst my many friends who was orphaned. Again and again I'd hear the same stories from them, the friends with parents in their seventies, the ones with parents in their eighties, their nineties—

*My father's complicated medical conditions require constant attention from me, but how do I adequately advocate for him 1,000 miles away?*

*My mother, who ran a successful business for thirty years, is really too confused to be handling her finances any more, but how do I take over those responsibilities for her without destroying her morale and self-esteem?*

*My father is struggling to keep house for himself since his second wife died: as the daughter, I am expected to fill in the empty spaces, though my judgement counts for little—it's my brother's opinion he listens to . . .*

*My father came to live with us after his stroke, but he's turning my already difficult juggling act into a nightmare: when he finishes yelling at the health care aides, he starts on me; when he's had it with me, he attacks my ten year old son . . .*

How do you strike a balance between meeting the needs and demands of an aging parent and the unrelenting pace of your own adult life? How do you walk the line between fulfulling the filial, moral responsibilities you feel and the dangers of overexposure to what may have been, even in better times, toxic parental relationships?

I see my friends responding as I did: we do the very best we can to be there as much as we possibly can, to be as helpful and loving and respectful as we possibly can. We try not to be consumed by the needs of our elderly parents, to continue to live our own lives with zest and with pleasure. We try to remember that we are separate from our parents, that we cannot change them or save them now any more than we ever could. We try not to be consumed by guilt.

# And then there's my father

When it seems as though
there's nothing left
to be depressed about,
I can always get depressed
about my father,
living alone in Florida,
eating out of cans.

He no longer goes out after dark,
he no longer drives a car,
no longer speaks on the phone in a storm
or watches while the TV is playing.
He no longer reads a book or a newspaper
or goes swimming in the pool.
He no longer invites a woman out to dinner
or gets a homecooked meal,
no longer sends anybody a birthday card
or goes to Temple on the holidays.
He no longer walks alone on the beach collecting shells.

At four in the morning
in my bed in New Jersey,
I lie awake and
think about my father.

My father died in 1989, shortly before I left the country for a sabbatical year in Israel. Having already experienced a year of mourning for a parent, I knew that I faced a difficult time. I tried to be gentle with myself that year, tender, nurturing. Tender. The way a loving parent is with a child. In effect, I renewed the process I'd embarked on after my mother's death—learning to parent myself.

One tactic was to give myself little treats: chief among those was time to write. There were other treats as well though, including the opportunity to spend a morning each week studying with a potter in Jerusalem. I learned to throw pots on the wheel, what pleasure. Mostly lots of mugs and little bowls—I never got to the level of proficiency of the other half dozen artisans in the studio, some of whom, like our teacher, were good enough to produce enormous platters, intricate ritual objects, dinnerware for twelve . . . But I was pretty good, good enough to give me pleasure in the work and in the product . . .

An odd consideration if you're working on the wheel—you need to keep your fingernails quite short. They can't grow longer than the fingertips themselves—otherwise they come between you and the clay and wreck havoc. So my hands looked different to me that year.

# Though I Stared Earnestly
# at my Fingernail

Yesterday when I was on the #7 bus
I happened to look at the cuticle of my right forefinger
and for a moment I thought not that it was mine
but that it was my father's—

the same small confusion I have from time to time
when I catch sight of my daughter
in her denim skirt, size 3
and I feel lean, willowy, in her clothes.

So there I was on the #7 bus
overtaken by a longing very close to love
staring at the cuticle of my right forefinger.
I remembered how clean and short he kept his nails

and suddenly there was the whole man
reconstituted from a fingernail
standing before me, smiling broadly
his face flushed with pleasure.

But then just as suddenly he was gone
and though I stared earnestly at my fingernail
I failed to bring him back.

Where can you go to find the love of your parents once they're gone? And from what daily tasks might the taste of the madelaine suddenly emerge?

When I was a child, my mother did our laundry by hand. Lines strung on pulleys crisscrossed from the windows of Brooklyn courtyard apartments, and when you were done with the washing, you hung the wash out on the line to dry.

After half an adulthood of suburban ease, I was startled, then seethed with resentment to discover that our Jerusalem apartment (like most) had laundry lines strung up, and that the job of hanging out the wash inevitably fell to me. But seething and resentment grow tiresome, more sensible to accept reality and make a game of it. My way of making a game of it was to figure out various systems of what best to hang where—where was the sun strongest to dry our heavy denim jeans, how to secure permapress shirts so the clothespins didn't leave wrinkles (clip them by the shirttails!). There's pleasure in a game well played, also time in mundane chores for the mind to travel, also the wonderful smell of Jerusalem captured in your socks, your blouses, your bedsheets.

# The Warmth of the Sun

My fingers were cold this morning
hanging out the wash
but the warmth of the sun
reminded me of how I had planned
to sit in the sun with my mother.

I was going to take off
from teaching in the spring
because she had leukemia
and I had just learned
I was pregnant.

I thought in the spring
I would go down to Florida
and we would sit together
in the sun.

But in November
on Thanksgiving Day
she died
before the spring
before the sun.

Then I sat on a hard
cardboard box sent over
by the Jewish undertaker
and I consoled myself
with many cigarettes
under the disapproving
eye of my sister-in-law.

In the twelfth week
I lost that baby.

All this happened so long ago
but still, even today
the warmth of the sun
reminds me of my mother.

This summer my friend Alice, along with her siblings and assorted family members, finally moved her parents out of the enormous Victorian home they had owned for more than forty years. Health problems this elderly couple faced made the move a necessity—countless stairs which could no longer be climbed, doorways too narrow for wheelchairs. Now her parents are adjusting to life in a retirement home.

But Alice's "summer vacation" was marked not only by constant hospital visits, but also by day after day of grueling work, sifting through the accrued possessions of not one but two people who threw nothing away. From the sublime to the ridiculous—four perfectly good toasters, the little plaster couple who had graced the top tier of their 1938 wedding cake.

No one puts themselves through such a physically demanding and emotionally wrenching ordeal unless a death or an impending move necessitates the work. Sadly, I have had several summers like the one my friend Alice just had. Each time a close relative dies and their home must be vacated, someone in the family is obliged to go through the "stuff" of their lives. You make piles—the piles to give to charity, the piles to throw away, the piles for other relatives and old friends, the piles you want to keep for yourself. I have several boxes of my father's 1920's law books, not because I will ever open them or use them or refer to them, but simply because I know how he went without lunches to buy those books when he put himself through law school and so these particular artifacts of his life have a certain holy status for me.

# In the attic

I am sitting on a wooden child's chair,
an old one bought for $2 when Littlebrook
School was closed for want of children.
Some days I sit on this little chair
for 8 or 9 hours and the hardness
hurts my ass more and more but I don't
change chairs because it's comfortable
to feel pain in a place as concrete as my ass.

I am spending this summer in my attic,
on a dig of sorts, a dig in my attic.
The layers go back to the beginning
of this century when my parents were born.
For the last few days I have lingered
in one of the boxes I brought back up
North after my father died.

I read every paper—the Valentine he sent
to her in 1931, the one she sent to him
in 1932; waiting to get married, waiting, waiting,
patience turning to anguish. I with 20/20 hindsight
know they will not marry till 1935 when there is
finally enough money for their own apartment.

All jumbled together I find the polite requests
(1932, 1934, 1936) he wrote to law professors
for references and then I find his check register
from 1989, a shaky hand betraying what
we have come to know as "silent strokes."
I am surprised, in this box, to find a card
announcing the birth of Merle Lizbeth, 6 pounds
7 ounces. I find the menu from my wedding dinner,
detailing "roast capon" and even "salted almonds."

Where I am going there is no attic.
I work to condense my father to a still
smaller box all the while trying
not to dishonor him.

I said earlier that the experience of lighting yahrzeit candles has changed for me over the years. In the beginning it brought back such a raw pain of loss that I dreaded the day, dreaded the candle.

As the years have gone on and the actual presence of my mother moves further and further away from me, I experience that "flickering little light" as her tangible presence in my home. After all these years I find myself looking forward to the day of her yahrzeit, looking forward to the special sense of her spirit in my home. The yahrzeit candle can light the way back through doorways in time, providing possibilities of openings.

# Yizkor

It's almost midnight
and I'm sitting here in the living room
keeping your yahrzeit candle company.
It's so many years now
I closed my eyes to remember
something real about you
and you know what I thought of?
I saw you ironing—
it was his underwear!

When I was a girl I wondered if someday
I'd love someone enough to iron his underwear.
Well, I've been married twenty years
and I love him very much
but I don't iron his underwear,
I don't even turn it right side out,
I don't even fold it,
I sort of stuff it in the drawer.
Truly I love him very much
but I still think what I thought when I was 11—
no one sees your underwear.

I'm all grown up now,
completely grown up now,
and still I don't get it—
no one sees your underwear.

I'm not being critical,
I'm not making fun,
it's just that we both have to face it—
I'm a different kind of wife.

You're gone,
and he's gone,
the foyer is gone,
the ironing board is gone,
and the underwear is gone.

All that remains is me,
sitting in this chair,
looking at the yahrzeit candle,
remembering.

Ironing underwear. How many people have told me since I wrote that poem their own memories of mother ironing underwear. And how many deep conversations have ensued because of that poem: conversations about the nature of love, duty, the housewife, mothers and daughters, the nature of underwear.

Recently I was away, giving a talk and a poetry reading. I was staying with an old, wonderful friend and asked her if I could throw my sweater in her dryer on "fluff" to get out the stubborn wrinkles it had acquired. Apparently "fluff" didn't work though and when I awoke in the morning it was to discover that Karen had ironed my sweater! So I read her the poem and we got to talking. She offered me another possibility: how intimate, to iron the clothing that touches the skin of your lover . . . Maybe you just needed to find your own ways of making erotic contact Merle . . . Maybe your daughter will find baking challah for her lover too conventional. Maybe she'll go back to ironing . . .

Going back. Many years ago (actually in the late '60s) Eddie asked a therapist friend of ours if he'd ever slept with a patient. Yes, Herman replied, that happens. We were dismayed—even in the permissive '60s, that seemed a violation. No, he laughed, I don't mean I have sex with them, I mean I literally sometimes fall asleep on them. When they're telling me what has for them become a mythic tale, what I call "an old tape"—"This and such happened when I was 12 and we were vacationing in Colorado and my father said . . . "—it's lost its energy, its truth, and it bores me, so that if the office is overheated and I'm tired, I'll doze off. It serves to tell me and the client that this story they've told a hundred times before is, or perhaps has become, devoid of true feeling. It's become instead an impediment to healing, to growth.

For years and years we go along telling everyone, most especially ourselves, the stories of our lives. Those same old stories, the same old tapes.

From time to time we need to reenter the facts of our lives, no matter how painful, no matter how terrifying, reenter the facts, stir them up in a new way . . . I'm at one of those times now.

# Going Back

I've gone back to my childhood
for a while. I'm going to
walk through the old rooms,
remember what my bedspread
looked like, remember how
my brothers scotch-taped
pictures of their sports idols
to the walls over their beds
like serious Catholics stick
up a crucifix for a child
to look at as he falls asleep.

What bizarre things you
remember. I'm going to walk
around that old apartment
and cry out loud all the tears
I swallowed as a child.
I'll cry, I'll cry, and when I'm
finally done I'll empty out
the old furniture, sweep
clean the floors. I'll feel
so light that the old habit
I've always had—the deep sighing—
that old habit will have
mysteriously disappeared.

# 7

*Israel*

I didn't want to spend a year in Israel.

When the kids were little and it gradually became clear that we weren't going to be able to send them to Hebrew day school, I had agreed with Eddie that we would do the next best thing for their Jewish education—spend a year living in Israel. In 1989 though, when Eddie's sabbatical came due and he began taking the concrete steps necessary to relocate in Jerusalem, it was at the height of the first intifada and I felt as if I'd made a pact with the devil.

First and foremost, I feared for our physical safety. But it was even more than that. I despised the policies of the Likud party in power, I didn't want to live in a country where women were so often second-class citizens (certainly to my way of thinking, in the religious hierarchy), I felt no ties there, and when my father died two months before we were to depart, I dreaded even more profoundly the thought of now spending a year of mourning cut off from all my closest friends. I had to be dragged to the plane.

The reality that confronted me was an utter and constant surprise. To begin with, on the most visceral level, I found I felt strangely at home, more at home than I had on my various earlier visits. Perhaps, as I reflect on it now, this deeper "at-homeness" was linked to my new reality as an orphan in the world.

# Here in Jerusalem

*for Lillian Uhrbach Lewis, 1910–1976*
*Milton Lewis, 1910–1989*


Here in Jerusalem,
a city she never saw
and he only once,
I feel so keenly
the presence of my mother,
the presence of my father.

Calling from the kitchen window
to my son who is playing ball
in the courtyard below,
carrying potatoes and apples,
detergent and tuna fish,
the bags so heavy I must stop
every few feet to catch my breath,
watching my wash flying on the line,
running with my daughter for the bus,

every day here I am thrust
back to the Brooklyn of 1957,
the Brooklyn which cradled me,
the Brooklyn which embarrassed me,
the Brooklyn of my childhood
which made a bit of sense.

And then the wind shifts—
the air on my cheek
the sun in my bones—
I close my eyes,
it is the Florida of their retirement,
I am a visitor in my parents' home.

Our skin hot and tight,
sand caught between our toes,
we tumble into the air-conditioned
darkness of their living room,
children together, perpetual holiday,
eagerly awaiting the next treat.

Where are my parents really?
haunting the three-room apartment in Brooklyn
where now some black or Puerto Rican family
dresses quickly on cold winter mornings?
or playing on Sun Coast white beaches
then waiting in line for the early bird special?
or quietly disappearing into the earth
of a Queens cemetery I numbly, rarely visit?

Or have they traveled with me,
surprised but open at last
to new adventures,
have they traveled with me
to spend this year
here in Jerusalem.

When we arrived in Jerusalem that August, I quickly renewed an old friendship with Veronika, a composer and music educator who, it turned out, had become a major driving force in a variety of peace initiatives. In fact, though she had a demanding full-time job, a husband, two children, and aging, ailing parents to care for, she seemed at times to be single-handedly manning the peace front. I was drawn to her warmth and the comfort of our deep friendship, drawn to her moral passion, and over the course of the year I too became, uncharacteristically, a political activist, traveling regularly with Veronika to the West Bank to meet with Palestinians, to participate in demonstrations, eventually even to become a leader of Israeli-Palestinian dialogue groups.

Though I did spend days exploring the treasures of Jerusalem, studied pottery with an Israeli ceramicist, was active in supporting religious Israeli feminists trying to secure equal rights to worship at the Wall, worked on a new play and made connections with the Israeli theatre community—and of course supervised the daily comings and goings of Lisa and Uri enrolled in an Israeli school—the real focus of my life that year was unquestionably my political involvement. That involvement had its beginnings in my emotional life as I imbibed the mood of the country and the city in which I was now living.

# Friday in Jerusalem

I feel a sadness today I can't name;
two challahs I bought this morning
and some cakes,
the week's used clothes are washed
and on the line,
many crisp autumn apples I soaked
in soapy water in the sink,
also grapes and tomatoes, a single yam.

I am tired of being sad,
tired of my own sadness,
I have no reason to be sad—
I have clothes to wear
and fruit to eat,
no one has bombed my house,
no one comes in the night to question my husband,
my son does not sit in jail awaiting charges.

I want to be happy
like the wet clothes on my washline
moving in the sunshine,
I want to be happy
like the green grapes clean grapes
slowly drying on my countertop,
I want to be as simple, as innocent,
as a small bunch of green grapes
or a clean sock drying on the line.

One of the very first weekly political activities I joined in was to stand with Women in Black. During the years of the intifada, as a protest to the Israeli occupation of the West Bank and Gaza, women stood in a square in downtown Jerusalem (other cities as well) every Friday from 1 to 2 P.M., dressed in black, holding signs in Hebrew, Arabic, or English which read, Stop the Occupation. I believe the choice of Friday as demonstration day was a purely practical one—in Israel many people get a half-day off on Friday, to allow them to prepare for Shabbat, and so they could be more readily available to participate. Aside from the practical logistics though, I think having such a public demonstration on Fridays served as a symbolic counterpoint: on Friday in Jerusalem it seems as though the entire city is engaged in washing its floors, selecting the tastiest challah, buying the most vibrant bouquet to grace the Shabbos table. It feels as though the city itself participates in a joyous countdown—Shabbos is coming! Shabbos is coming! So the demonstration cast a shadow on the city's anticipated celebration of Shabbat as the Occupation cast a shadow on the moral spirit of a struggling, still-young democracy.

Going to stand with Women in Black each Friday epitomized a profound change in me, not unlike the profound change of crossing over the border from not-being-a-mother to being-a-mother. (Norman Frimer had once remarked to Eddie and me that he thought the greatest shift in identity came not when a person who was single got married, but rather when a person who was not a parent became a parent.) And just as becoming a mother was transformative beyond all reckoning or preparation, I became a new Merle when I stood with Women in Black.

There really were two different experiences involved in the commitment, first, the standing there, and second, the coming and going. Although it was a bit of a physical challenge standing at a vigil in the heat of the Middle Eastern day dressed in a color that attracts and magnifies the heat, I soon discovered that supporters walked up and down the lines of protestors offering us bottles of water. Sometimes people also

146

circulated with bags of dried fruit, and most every week there was a gentle looking laborer who gifted each of us with a shy smile and a rose. But from my perspective, the real contribution of these supporters was their implicit effort to offset the effect of right-wing taxi drivers and other opponents of the peace movement who periodically would menacingly whiz by shouting profanities. I am at heart a modest person and though I joked that an auxiliary bonus of my political activity was the weekly enhancement of my limited Hebrew by the colorful new vocabulary I was acquiring (*zonot*, prostitutes, chief among the epithets), still I was truly shaken by the verbal violence of the many who drove past us, and the subliminal threat of violence reflected in their enraged faces, faces contorted by hatred.

Even more disturbing to me though were the white- and blue-clad counterdemonstrators across the street who often shouted at us as they waved oversize Israeli flags. Each Friday, inwardly timid and uncertain, I trembled as they accused me of disloyalty to a country I loved, each Friday challenged me anew to rethink with great care step by step from the beginning what I believed about the Occupation, what I believed and why—that it was the Occupation that raised a threat of ultimate peril, not the protest to it. Each week the counterdemonstrators and the palpable hatred of some who drove by us challenged me to go through the process all over again, my stomach churning, never to feel utterly absolutely certain, because being merely human I can never have absolute moral certainty. And so I felt the repeated necessity of making a *hesbon ha nefesh*, an accounting of the soul, to account to myself for why I was standing there. When I was finished, I gained strength from the many others with whom I stood.

And then there was the coming and going to the demonstration square on the bus each week, and that was another matter, for that was accomplished solo. I felt like a target, an advertisement on Fridays in Jerusalem, dressed all in black, especially during the many hot months when there was no thought of wearing a jacket or shirt as overlay to disguise my black "uniform" and my politics. I did, in the many months of

147

Middle Eastern summer heat, take to wearing a colorful scarf, but I felt always en route that every eye could identify me anyway and my heart pounded wondering what the consequence of that vulnerability might be. It did cross my mind to wear something "safe," and maneuver a change of wardrobe when I reached my destination, but I couldn't face the cowardice of that, and most deeply of all, it was more painful to admit that I might be at serious risk from my fellow Jews—Israelis on the right—than to brave a potential attack. So I traveled the city each Friday morning doing my pre-Shabbos errands with a subliminal sense of vulnerability until I reached the square at 1 P.M., and then again at 2 when I took the bus back home to finish preparing for Shabbat. All in all, Women in Black was the frame for a private and public, psychic and political, metamorphosis.

Prior to August 1989, I often had described myself as "the most apolitical person I know." I don't think that I was self-centered, or blind to the suffering of others. It had to do with the *New York Times.*

When I was growing up in Brooklyn, my mother didn't read the *New York Times,* the most serious newspaper, the paper with important news of the world. In the evenings, when she finally had an opportunity to sit down and relax a little, she read instead the afternoon edition of the *World Telegram and Sun,* a paper that included Dear Abby, recipes, human interest stories, and a page of comic strips in the back. From this I learned that the affairs of the world are complicated, dense, beyond the capabilities of women. From this I learned that women are not political. For some years into adulthood even, the palpable anxiety I felt when faced with a page of Hebrew letters was the same palpable anxiety I felt when faced with the front page of the news section of the *New York Times.* I can't do this, this is for grown-ups, this is for men.

The question of class identity also comes into play here. In my formative high school years it felt as though there was an inner circle of honors students who were politically involved, the students who joined school clubs devoted to the important social causes of the day, working toward nuclear disarmament, fighting manifestations of racism in America. They dressed a certain way, they talked a certain way, they were headed for the Ivy League, and though we were peers and equals in the classroom, I couldn't afford the kinds of clothes they wore, I was mystified and intimidated by their easy social grace, their sense of entitlement. I felt frozen out of their world, not good enough to be a part of their political activism, and so not good enough to be politically active.

The changes in me wrought by my new Israeli reality were twofold: for the first time I had a model, a mentor, of political activism and she was a woman. Veronika had the energy of five people, was absolutely devoid of fear, and was fanatical in her commitment to peace and justice. Second, this was the first time in my life I had the opportunity to come face to face with what I often struggled to fathom in the pages of the *Times.* As powerfully as I had been acculturated as a woman not to understand political issues, I had also been acculturated as a woman to notice actual people, to listen to them, to feel for them, to try to help them. And wherever I went now as I traveled the West Bank, I saw on people's faces the ravages of the Occupation. Their suffering and desperation cried out to me. Moreover, in the economic strictures of the simplest of their lives, I often recognized myself. The poorest of them were living the genteel poverty of my childhood. I felt at home in their homes.

In the early days of our sabbatical year, I had not yet established ties with Palestinians in dialogue groups, the ongoing relationships which eventually would become the center of my Israel experience. Within a few weeks of our arriving though, having settled Lisa and Uri into a network of activities and friends, I began a kind of apprenticeship under Veronika's wing, tagging along, listening, watching, as she went about her rounds. One of the earliest of what were to be countless visits with her to the West Bank was a trip to the small town of Hal Hul. This particular expedition came at the request of some local residents—a girl's school had been teargassed by Israeli soldiers, some students required hospitalization, and a call went out to members of the peace movement to come demonstrate by their presence that there were Israelis who cared about these children.

I wondered in the early morning, as I hastily prepared to leave my Jerusalem apartment, if there was anything appropriate to bring my hosts to warm, to soften, the atmosphere I potentially anticipated. Not food, not flowers, I thought, and suddenly I settled on a pocket-size double picture frame with school photos of Lisa and Uri, grades five and one, respectively. A few hours later, standing in the school yard surrounded by clusters of elementary-aged schoolgirls, the smiling innocence of my own children served as a kind of passport to connection with these Palestinian children who saw me as a mother and were eager to practice their limited English asking about the children in the photographs.

Later that morning I sat together with the group of Israelis with whom I had made the trip as we were joined by some of the children's mothers, teachers, and one or two town officials. Most of these traditional, rural Palestinian women spoke little English though, and while the fact of our visit had made its intended point, and they welcomed us appreciatively, passing bowls of just-picked grapes from backyard arbors, it seemed to me there was a lot of awkward silence. In the aftermath of that visit, I made an early attempt to give these women a voice, to reach behind the smiles, the handshakes, to imagine what they were thinking. The speaker in the following poem is a Palestinian woman modeled on the women I met that morning in Hal Hul.

# The Visit

You come. You go. You come and go. I see you.

I see you come and go. Thank you for coming.

You come to help, I know. Thank you for coming.

We are surprised you come to help. We are surprised

you are kind. You smile, you are kind, we are surprised.

You smile, you say "This land is beautiful."

You are surprised this land is beautiful. We know.

We are not surprised. You come. You come and go.

You smile and we smile. You come. You smile, we smile.

Thank you for coming. You come to help, we know.

You come, you smile, we smile. We are tired now.

We are tired of smiling. Soon, we hope, you will go.

The next West Bank visit found me packing a bag lunch and my bottle of water to travel to East Jerusalem where a small group of Israelis shared an Arab taxi to a military base outside Nablus (under curfew) to be observers at the Beita trial. Beita was the village on the West Bank where a group of settler high school kids went on a Pesach hike and clashed with some local youths. When the dust settled, one Palestinian boy and one Israeli girl lay dead, both shot by the same over-wrought Israeli guard. Twenty-three villagers were subsequently arrested and, over the course of the next year and a half, held in prison awaiting trial, mostly for stone throwing. A commit-tee of Israelis formed, first to provide the accused with a law-yer, then to rebuild the many homes in Beita demolished illegally by the Army in the aftermath of the original tragedy. I arrived in the country soon after the trials had begun, at a time when members of the Beita Committee were traveling to sit as interested observers at the trials of the villagers they had come to know.

We arrive at the military base and join a large number of local men and women milling around the outside of the fence, waiting for sight of a brother, waiting for a word with a son's lawyer, waiting to find someone who might take the case of a newly arrested husband. Waiting. First a man and then a woman approach Veronika to ask for help. They talk quietly in turn, the man writing down some phone numbers Veronika offers. I am incredulous—they know of her, they know to trust her, even more remarkable, she knows how to help them. We wait to be admitted to the base, finally single-file, we show our passports, we are in.

We, myself and a dozen or so Israelis from the Beita Committee, mostly sit together in the far back. In front of us in the small hot courtroom are the relatives and neighbors of the accused. The men and women from Beita sit separately, the men on the benches to the left of the aisle, the women on the benches to the right. The women are wearing large white head coverings. As I view this scene from a back bench I could almost feel myself in synagogue. Veronika, sitting up front with the village women, shares a bag of fruit she has brought. The beautiful young wife of one of the accused, a girl with an open shining face, sits next to her, smiling, talking, her arm linked through Veronika's. I keep looking from one face to the other, both faces framed by head coverings—younger/older, Palestinian/Jew—yet they could easily have passed for sisters.

The visit to Hal Hul, the visit to Nablus to observe the Beita trial, these are among the first of countless excursions to the West Bank that I will make over the course of the year for grassroots meetings and "activities" as Veronika and her peace colleagues term them, activities to foster understanding, to bridge bitterness and despair, to create and deepen connections between Israelis and Palestinians. And always with the added goal of shedding light on cooperation between the two peoples, shedding light on Palestinians who are indeed partners for peace but who have been rendered invisible by a government and its media that seem to work with a vengeance to keep them invisible. Many times during this intifada year I am present with Israelis and Palestinians at joint peaceful demonstrations, activist projects to which the media has been invited but then in the end does not attend. We keep throwing parties but nobody shows up to file a report, to conduct an interview, to take a picture.

By the middle of the year, Veronika, overwhelmed by the responsibilities of running a number of Israeli-Palestinian dialogue groups throughout the West Bank and in Jerusalem, as well as jointly conceiving and creating a considerable array of grassroots demonstrations and activities, asked my help in organizing and facilitating a special dialogue group for women in Beit Sahur, a West Bank suburb of Bethlehem. The women in this town had been participating in Israeli-Palestinian dialogue groups together with their husbands, brothers, friends, but felt it was hard to get a word in with the men often shouting over their voices, and so the Palestinian women asked to have separate dialogue groups with their female counterparts to more easily speak and be heard. (Having myself frequently attended some of these dialogue groups with men and women,

I had in fact been fascinated by the interactions between Israeli men and women and Palestinian men and women, especially watching husbands and wives on both sides jockeying for airtime; the marital wrestling was much the same on both sides, though the Israeli women by and large were more comfortable and successful than the Palestinian women at insisting on their fair share of time to talk.)

The town of Beit Sahur had a history from early on in the intifada of nonviolent demonstrations against the Israeli occupation: among other strategies of protest, these Palestinians organized a tax strike in town. Taking their lead from the heroes of the American Revolution, they declared, "No taxation without representation!" refusing to pay taxes to the Israeli government without enjoying the full benefits of citizenship, including a vote in how their tax money could be spent. (This principled tax strike resulted in the confiscation of large quantities of private household and business goods from Beit Sahur citizens, property taken in lieu of tax money, property that languished in hangers at Ben Gurion airport, and was eventually auctioned off to Israeli buyers for a pittance of their worth to yield government revenue and to punish the Palestinian resistors.) These confiscations, though causing real hardship to many, did not dissuade or interrupt the nonviolent approach of Beit Sahur. From the beginning, their way of protesting the Occupation had been nonviolent and that protest continued with the multiplication of dialogues with Israelis.

When Veronika asked me to take a leading role in organizing this women's dialogue group, I felt conflicted. I wanted very much to work with these women, to be of help in moving both sides even a small step closer toward the communication and mutual understanding that we all hoped would prepare the way to peace, but I also had grave misgivings about taking a central role. I was after all an outsider, a visitor, I would be going back home at the end of the year and so my children were not at risk in the long-term ways that either the Israeli or Palestinian children were at risk. Wouldn't both sides see my participation as interference and resent me? Perhaps most of all though, I was terrified of taking responsibility—surely there was someone who could do this more skillfully, more successfully. But if there was, she didn't volunteer, and women on both sides urged me to help. After some reflection, I concluded I hadn't the right to say no.

The Israeli women who participated in the dialogues, dialogues that would be ongoing for the next number of months, were in their thirties and forties—an editor, some teachers, a therapist, an artist, a nurse, some women home with babies. The Palestinians in the group, spanning fully three generations, were both Christian and Muslim, and represented as well a wider socioeconomic spread than the Israelis did—some, educated professionals—teachers, lab technicians, businesswomen—others, pillars of the community but without Western-style credentials. We met every other week, for many months, each time in a different woman's home in Beit Sahur, and that afforded us a special view into the diversity of their individual lives.

Each time the women lined up to greet us, each time the same etiquette of serving was observed: bowls of nuts on the table with many glass ashtrays to catch the shells, juice served at once, then toward the end of the meeting small cups of ink black Turkish coffee and glasses of *nana*—mint tea.

Unlike other groups we knew of who had what seemed to us a bizarre rule that anything *but* politics was open for discussion, we got right in there—no subject was taboo. There was anger, there were tears, there were often accusations, often hostility and pain. Many times, on both sides, we would secretly vow, "I'm not going back there." Some participants did in fact drop out or take a breather for a few weeks. But most women stuck with it and tried hard to listen.

Both sides talked about their lives under the Occupation, the Israelis about their right to be in this land, about the anguish of sending off husbands and children to soldier (in the early months of our meeting, there were not yet the horrifying incidents of terrorism that came later in the year and that focused

155

later meetings). I will never forget one Palestinian woman at our first meeting telling us of her adolescent son and daughter: "The streets are raising our children, the soldiers are raising our children, the stones are raising our children, we are not raising our children." This was clearly the topic of most concern to them—the random violence their children breathed in day by day, the hatred that the occupiers engendered in their youngsters, their fear at their own gradual loss of parental authority. In fact, some of the most powerful emotional exchanges occurred between the mothers in the group. Once an Israeli mother whose son was serving in the Army and had just completed his first tour of duty, described how he came home for that first leave and how she and her husband spent the night sitting up with their son as he cried and told stories of what it was like for him to be an occupier. The Palestinians in the room sat in uncomprehending silence, trying to imagine an Israeli soldier crying.

Interestingly, the mothers of younger children on both sides reported remarkable commonalities in the effects of the political situation on their offspring. Both sides told of persistent bed-wetting, beyond the age when it is usual for children to wet the bed. Both sides described their children suffering from disturbed sleep, nightmares night after night. And both sides, when speaking of their teenagers, shared stories of an inability to plan for a future—these teens felt no confidence that they would survive to reach adulthood and if they did, was there hope of a future for which to plan? Again and again, the women sat incredulously as their own words came from the lips of the other side.

Often we had a scheduled topic for the meeting, sometimes crises offered their own topics, as on the day we went to visit the brother of Najah, a Palestinian member of our group. She told us he was gravely ill (though she didn't explain the cause or source of his condition), she just said she wanted us to meet him and to hear his story; I think she also wanted him to meet us. We, the Israeli women and I, went, because Najah had become our friend and also because it's a mitzvah to visit the sick.

# Bikur Cholim

Before our dialogue today
we are going to visit Najah's brother—
he was shot last week
passing through a checkpoint.

It was dark and raining hard,
he didn't see, didn't hear,
didn't know to stop.
The bullet traveled through
the car door, through
the driver's seat, into
his back, down down
to his spleen.

The soldiers pulled him
from the car,
stripped him naked,
they stood him against a wall,
blood coming from his back,
from his mouth,
in the dark rain
naked.

A passing officer saw,
yelled to the soldiers
*Are you crazy?*
so they took him
to the military police,
and finally finally,
after double checking
that he had absolutely no record,
to the hospital.

Ten Jewish women—an intifada minyan—
troop through his living room
crowded with friends and neighbors
paying a sick call on Mahmoud,
an ordinary man,
a gentle looking man,
suddenly with many strange women
standing vigil around his bed.

He tells us his story,
in the middle of the telling
his wife rejoins us,
passing a basket
of gaily wrapped candies—
you can't say no,
it would be an insult.
The story is coming to an end.

*Slicha,* he says, *Slicha*—
it seems that after Mahmoud
engaged an Israeli lawyer
the soldiers came to the hospital
and said *Slicha*—
*now you should drop the case*—
*we said Slicha.*

We wish Mahmoud a speedy recovery,
troop out again through the living room
past the gathering of friends and neighbors—
*What? You are not staying for coffee?*
No, we can't, we will coffee with
the women of our dialogue group,
today we will talk about
What are Our Sources of Information and
How Do We Know What We Know and
How Do We Decide What is True.

I leave Mahmoud's house and walk
into the gray February muddy sky,
still in the palm of my hand
a gaily wrapped candy.

From time to time in the next months we would ask our friend how her brother was doing. He was in and out of hospital, always with pain, with mysterious fever, needing yet another surgery. The Israeli lawyer who took the case told me he doubted anything would ever come of it, but that one had to pursue these things nonetheless. He said he spoke to the two soldiers—"They're boys, the age of my son, boys with guns." He wanted them to visit the family, to meet this man's wife and two young children, to see what they had done, but the Palestinian family refused.

In March, a call from the women in Beit Sahur: Would we like to join them in a demonstration on International Women's Day? They warn that it may prove dangerous, but I have become a regular on the West Bank, a regular in this town overlooking Bethlehem, and I figure, as usual, if they're willing, I'm willing. A dozen of us arrive and join in the march— a hundred of them, two hundred of them—young girls in jeans, old women in traditional dress, many friends from the dialogue. Up and down the streets we wind, carrying banners, singing; a few of them hold aloft small pieces of fabric—red, green, black, and white—national colors, illegal colors. The march itself is illegal—the gathering, the banners, the songs. We turn a corner and there at the bottom of the hill is an Israeli patrol. Maybe they don't see that we are just women singing, that we are unarmed. First they fire tear gas. Everyone expected this, but still it is unpleasant. The crowd does not disperse. Then suddenly, plastic bullets, and we all start running. Into a courtyard, down a long flight of stone steps. My heart is beating very fast, but at the same time I'm standing outside myself, calmly observing: "I'm capable of being more frightened than this." The tear gas, I am told, will linger in the air for the next few days, but within an hour we—the Israelis— are in a taxi driving back to Jerusalem. One of the women in our group is clutching a plastic bullet she picked up from the ground. She shows it to her husband when she gets home. She brings it to synagogue with her. She cannot seem to stop shaking. She doesn't come back to dialogue.

In April some of us go to the Russian Compound where a teenage Palestinian neighbor of Judith is having a preliminary hearing, held but not yet charged with setting a bomb in Mahane Yehuda, the Jerusalem marketplace. His elderly mother is beside herself under the strain of this first-time separation from her youngest child. When he is brought into the hallway, she falls on him with kisses and tears. The prosecutor shouts angrily at her that this is not permitted, this is not a visit. To those who know him, the boy looks terrible. One Israeli runs next door to bring him hot coffee, also coffee for the guard. The guard urges him to drink the warm liquid, to drink the second cup as well. Veronika, seeing he is cold, goes off to a corner for a moment. She comes back with her pullover sweater in hand. Grateful, he puts it on; had he noticed she was wearing it, he would not have accepted. My mind races, what do I have to contribute? Then suddenly I smile to myself, it is Friday. The two challahs I bought for Shabbat are still warm in the bag in my hand. To offer a whole loaf would shame him. I begin tearing off pieces, which he rapidly devours. His hunger abated a bit, he begins to enjoy the sweetness of the warm bread, the novelty of the plump raisins. The guards smile knowingly at my offering; they encourage him to eat. They are tired of being the enemy.

In fact, that spring there were in rapid succession a spate of terrorist attacks on Israelis, including a bombing and several attempted bombings in Mahane Yehuda where weekly I did my grocery shopping, often with my eleven-year-old daughter and my seven-year-old son in tow. The same week of the marketplace bombing there was also a guerilla attack on the beach at Nitzanim. When I came to the next dialogue, the Palestinian women began defending the assault on Nitzanim, doing their best to avoid taking moral responsibility for violence—"Those who carried out the attack weren't going to kill *people,* they were intending to kill *soldiers.*" The meeting became particularly stormy as of course the Israelis present argued that it was a meaningless distinction in a country where everyone needs to serve in the Army, where Army service is necessary for survival. I then related to the group my recent narrow escape in Mahane Yehuda: in fact, I was headed to shop the day of the bombing and only because my bus was slow did I arrive a few seconds after the explosions which tore into the very restaurant where I normally parked Lisa and Uri to enjoy their beloved *svarma* as I did my grocery shopping. My Palestinian friends were stunned, shaken, their bluster of defensiveness dissolved. Such was often the rhythm of dialogue—angry accusations, back and forth, back and forth, then when anger finally exhausted itself, a quiet sharing of mutual sorrow.

Perhaps because I spent that transformative year in Israel not as an isolated, discrete individual, but as the mother of a young family—and therefore became a part of the fabric of two cultures and came to know in my daily routine so many mothers, so many children—my connections to these complex political problems were and have remained visceral. I know in my bones how parents on both sides cherish their children, how precious are the lives, the young bodies, of these children.

# A beautiful shining face

There was another bomb.
At the bus stop. My bus stop.
My neighbor's son was on his way to school.
He's 8. He's a dreamer, always late.
He imagines he's a knight, an astronaut.
This month he's a soccer star.

He's very bright
with a beautiful shining face.
There was a shower of glass
from the bomb.
He looked up at the noise
and the glass from the store window—
all in his face.

Yes, he's alive
but he will need a new face
and he has lost his sight.

He's at home. He won't go out.
His face is still bandaged.
His schoolmates come, by twos.
They bring him little treasures.
They are afraid, but they come.
They won't give up on him.

The end of our sabbatical year fell at the same time as *Tisha B'Av*, the solemn fast day which mourns the destruction of the first and second Temples in Jerusalem. I heard some friends complain as they labored to prepare the special chanting for the day from *Echa*, the Book of Lamentations—how can we continue each year to mourn a Temple we in fact don't want rebuilt—and I suddenly knew with perfect clarity what the day meant for me.

# Tisha B'Av

Together we sit on the ground
and mourn for the peace of Jerusalem,
like the treasure we each wanted—
we pulled and we pulled,
you pulled and I pulled,
and yes, of course,
finally we succeeded
in pulling it apart.

We watched together
as it fell to the ground
and smashed at our feet,
tears sprang to my eyes,
tears to yours,
each
separately
longing to undo the moment,
to walk backwards into the past,
to undo the moment,
the moments of pulling,
to walk backwards into the past
to the moment when
we could have shared
or taken turns
or something.

Come my friend
(for haven't we become friends after all
sharing our intimate
our primal pain)
come my friend,
come sit with me on the ground,
let us heap ashes on each other,

gently tenderly
I will teach you the melody
of my *Echa*,
together we will sit on the ground
and mourn for the peace of Jerusalem.

Leaving Israel was one of the most wrenching experiences of my life. In a single year I had made this country, this city, my home. Not just through my political activities, but through the ordinary day-to-day ways we cleave to a place—being befriended by neighbors, being welcomed into a synagogue community, coming to know local merchants and the parents of my children's schoolmates, coming to love the neighborhoods, the vistas, the very stones.

I did in the last weeks begin to carry a camera around with me, but since I couldn't admit to myself that this was the last time in the shuk, this was my last visit to the Old City, this was my last lunch with my cousin, many of those pictures I missed even though the camera was loaded and at hand. Other pictures I didn't take because I felt shy realizing how much these ordinary shots meant to me—the young French Jew from whom I'd bought my tuna fish and toilet paper all year; the sixtyish Jew from Syria who sold me beans and pasta and who after a mere six months had finally begun to smile when I entered his shop; and especially Sasson, my favorite of the four brothers who owned our corner grocery, who in his late twenties still dreamed of becoming a rock star, passing many a gray or sunny afternoon playing demo tapes of himself as he sat tending the checkout counter.

Most of all I wanted to take pictures of my friends in Beit Sahur, but after Veronika questioned whether or not they'd be comfortable with that and whether it would endanger them, I thought better of it. Even without her reservations, could I really have asked them to all stand together and smile at me as if this was the last day of camp?

The irony was, I realized, as I shopped for presents to bring home to the States, the year of intense political activity on behalf of the Israeli peace movement had made me feel closer than I had ever before felt to Israel. The irony was that a year of this work had made me into a Zionist. Wasn't I one before? Yes, certainly, in the sense that I supported the right of the state to exist, in the sense that I gave to UJA. But no, not in the sense that it had ever before hurt me physically to get on a plane and leave.

Our last morning, waiting for the ride to the airport, I sat on my bed in our Jerusalem apartment, struggling to come to terms with the pain of separation, separation not just from friends, from intricate networks of many friends, but from a city and a way of life.

# This poem is about a city

I came to you in a dream.
For many days and many nights
I circled you, watching.
Then slowly slowly
I began to taste you,
I lost myself in you,
freely tasting—
my hungry mouth
my hungry eyes—
I filled myself with you.
Gently with my fingers
I traced your old scars
and the new ones,
the angry red new ones.
Trembling knowingly
I gave myself to you.

But now the morning has come,
I rise up,
find on the floor
my old clothes.
Slowly slowly
I walk away.

# 8

*Repairing the World:*
*The Work of Tikkun Olam*

Living in Israel changed everything. I never imagined how profoundly and in what unexpected ways this sabbatical year would have transformed me. I had never before experienced the relentless intensity of political activism, for all intents and purposes, living in a war zone. Coming back to America, I missed the almost daily stimulating reality of life writ large—demonstrations, dialogues, the stark exotic beauty of desert landscapes, the passionate encounters with people clamoring to be heard as if their lives depended on it. Their lives did and do depend on it. I understood finally that responding to the important moral and ethical issues of the era in which I live, and thinking creatively about how I could participate in the work of tikkun olam, "the repair of the world," was my unavoidable responsibility as an adult. The spiritual and practical challenge of the next many years of my life would broaden now to include the struggle, the search, to find venues in which I could live out the moral imperative to be sharing in this ongoing work of repair. But that's a story that unfolded over the course of time.

In the weeks following our return to America, we suffered culture shock from all sides—we had become accustomed to an Israeli way of life, a simpler way of life, doing our daily shopping in a small corner grocery store that had all the necessities but not much more. I remember the first trips to the supermarket after we returned to Princeton, the shock at American abundance and privilege, standing immobile when I would turn the corner with my shopping cart and stand facing a gauntlet, flanked on two sides by a long long aisle with nothing but breakfast cereal. I would come home from grocery shopping emotionally drained, numb; I'd need to take a nap.

Sometimes my longing for things Israeli was intense. One of the things I missed most of all was the shuk, Mahane Yehuda. (I was delighted once to read somewhere that it was also a favorite place of Yehuda Amichai, a poet whose work I have long admired.) A Jerusalem landmark, its wares reflect the changing seasons as well as the holiday cycle—purple plums in the fall, *soufganiot* (fried doughnuts) for Hanukah, *hamantashen* (traditional triangular filled pastries) for Purim. The narrow lanes overflow with the breadth and breath of humanity, the ears are assailed by hundreds of peddlers who cry out with the prices for their grapes, their eggplants, their tomatoes.

# Exile

There at Pesach
in the shuk
they have mountains
of chocolate-covered macaroons
and by the shovelful
they give you as much
as you could want—
they sell it by the kilo.
You don't mind so much
the dirt on the floor,
the crowd pushing you from behind,
that's part of why you shop there—
to be with other people,
other people who need a good price.

Here in the ShopRite
with Barry Manilow and Bette Midler
in the background
in careful rows
are the 10 oz. cans of macaroons
and even though you read
the warning, "some settling
of contents may have occurred
during handling," every year
you are surprised anew
when you get it home and open
the can—you read the warning
but still you feel cheated
every time to open the can
and see it's half empty.

On my return to the States I began work on a new play whose themes grew out of my political activism in Israel. Though I knew in the midst of facilitating dialogue I didn't have the luxury to be listening with an ear for character and plot, once home and sitting at my writing desk, the people I had met and the stories I had heard echoed in my playwright's ear and in my heart. The play, *Across the Jordan*, subsequently published in the first anthology of Jewish women playwrights, *Making a Scene* (Syracuse University Press, 1997) explores the relationship between Daphna, a young Israeli lawyer assigned her first pro bono case, and her client, Najah, a Palestinian student accused of a terrorist bombing. The two women struggle to understand each other, to trust each other, and finally to learn to work together. This contemporary action takes place against an ancient backdrop of the biblical story of Sarah, Abraham, and Hagar.

Writing has often proved to be one way in which I can participate in the work of tikkun olam, taking readers down new roads they would otherwise be too fearful to travel. In writing this play I wanted to give audiences entrée into the complex moral world in which I had been privileged to live for a while: How can we dare to trust each other? How can we not?

I worked on the play, on new poems and essays, took advantage of every opportunity to speak to American audiences about the dialogues I had witnessed and to share the hopes they represented for a vision of peace and justice. Eventually, without noticing, I resumed the rhythms of life in America, became accustomed once again to large supermarkets; my son lost a few teeth and grew new ones, my daughter began to menstruate. But no sooner had we readjusted to life in Princeton, we decided to move to New York for new career opportunities. Amidst all the settling and resettling, we were thrilled to be able to return to Israel for several summers of teaching and research.

In Israel the landscape kept changing as well. The euphoria of handshakes, peace talks, treaties, normalization of neighborly relations. And then, assassination.

# On the death of Yitzchak Rabin

Old soldiers aren't supposed to die,
they're supposed to slowly fade away,
but ours is a new country, a small country,
and we must be parsimonious with everything,
even our old soldiers.

We cannot afford to retire our old soldiers,
we can't relegate them to corners, to rockers,
to retelling the stories of their glories
and their wounds.

We need them still on the front lines,
in the front row, we need them
standing up for us
while they have strength left to stand.

Even when we tear at them,
even when we curse them, piling insults,
calling traitor, traitor,
we need to squeeze all our resources,
wring harvests from parched earth, from desert.

We don't let go of our old soldiers, we shake
them by the throat, we choke them,
we make them cry, sinking to their knees
calling out for peace.

Opportunities for us to spend time in Israel began dwindling. Living in New York now, I looked around at my new home and what I saw on every street corner were desperately poor women and men, begging for spare change, huddled against buildings in the rain and the snow, sleeping in the streets at night.

I began working for Beyond Shelter, a coalition of the diverse and numerous synagogues on Manhattan's West Side that does advocacy and fundraising on behalf of low-income and homeless New Yorkers of all faiths and races. My efforts on behalf of this population in the city of my childhood spoke to several needs at once—a desire to alleviate the immediate suffering, a determination to affect the course of future policy-making, the impulse to reach back into my own history and bring some healing to that impoverishment, and finally, the kindling of a fragile hope that the kind of work I had done in Israel in what is after all a small world and so easier to maneuver as an activist, could also find parallel possibilities for effective organizing in the vast and therefore daunting country that is my own.

Beyond Shelter was founded by a group of laypeople who were active in their respective synagogue social action committees. They met originally while serving as volunteers in the few local shelters that existed for New York's homeless: they sought to compensate for inadequate staffing of shelters by themselves staying overnight on a rotating basis. Seeing how woefully inadequate those homeless shelters were, they came to understand that this terrible social crisis needed more serious, substantial solutions—in particular, the underlying policy issues needed to be addressed—and so they established an organization that could offer appropriate long-term help.

New York's low-income housing stock had deteriorated over decades: landlords who owned rent controlled buildings were sometimes unable, sometimes merely unwilling, to invest in necessary repairs, and eventually a building would deteriorate to the point of being uninhabitable (though tenants, having nowhere else to go, remained in these squalid apartments). The landlord might stop paying taxes to the city and the city would seize the property in lieu of that tax income, but the city was no better at providing services and desperately needed repairs. When a building was literally falling down, the city would condemn it, level it, and make way for new housing, except the new housing was generally of the most lucrative, luxury sort and the old tenants were then finally out on the street.

Beyond Shelter saw as its mission the preservation and reclamation of what was an alarmingly shrinking stock of affordable housing—through that preservation and reclamation they reasoned they could stem the tide of evictions and so prevent further homelessness. In part this was accomplished by fundraising for a revolving no-interest/low-interest loan fund to which low-income householders could apply to get money to fix an old but still salvageable boiler, to repair broken windows or antiquated plumbing.

A second thrust of the organization was to engage in educating the public and the West Side's rabbinic leadership about the city's crisis of homelessness and the root causes of that crisis, not insignificantly striving to dispel existing prejudices against the homeless that serve to further disempower and disenfranchise them. The rabbis of large and not so large, wealthy and not so wealthy, Conservative, Orthodox, Reform, Reconstructionist, and Renewal congregations began meeting together for discussions, briefings, brainstorming sessions, and site visits to see housing that Beyond Shelter had helped support and renovate. The involvement of the rabbis was crucial and impressive, modeling for congregants in this densely Jewish neighborhood what the demands of social justice were.

I worked for Beyond Shelter as their sole [modestly] paid staff person, with responsibilities that included organizing the ongoing work of the rabbis; setting up community-wide information sessions, lectures and briefings; implementing the decisions of the devoted and hardworking lay board; and grant writing. I learned so much: about homelessness, about indifference, devotion, bureaucracy, grant writing. And I discovered something that has informed my social justice activism ever since, something I discuss with people who seek me out to talk about how they can become involved in the work of tikkun olam: in choosing a project, one needs to consider more than the first question, namely, is this a cause I believe in. The second question needs to be, do the actual tasks of this work engage my particular strengths, talents, gifts, because if they don't, burnout will sooner or later regrettably hamper your effectiveness. No matter how worthy or noble the cause, if it doesn't engage your particular talents and thus give you periodic satisfaction and pleasure, the commitment will finally be impossible to sustain. Over the years I have come to understand my activism as existing in two categories—issues or organizations that offer opportunities for my personal engagement, and those I support financially by underwriting the hands-on work of others. Some combination of these two strikes a balance that fulfills my longing to help build a better world. At Beyond Shelter I learned that, yes, I could do grant writing, I could even do it pretty well, I could do administration, I could do it very well, but after two years I had to acknowledge that there was insufficient pleasure in the actual work that made up my day, day after day, and ultimately I couldn't continue.

I went back to writing, in fact, writing what turned out to be the first edition of this book. And the book has propelled many a journey since, often quite naturally and seamlessly enabling me to resume long-standing activist commitments, and also to develop new kinds of activist work, some of it emerging from the process of writing that has so nourished me over the years and the teaching of that process to others. I am fervent in my belief that a personal writing practice can help ground us in our lives, illuminate our life's experiences, reveal the new paths on which we need to journey, and allow us to speak deeply and authentically with one another and so satisfy the hunger we all feel for connection. I have pioneered this spiritual writing practice, have shared it over the last years with a variety of constituencies, including rabbis, rabbinical students, lay leaders, spiritual seekers of all stripes. And it would, unexpectedly, lead me back to work once again with peace seekers from the Middle East.

As time passed, opportunities to engage in dialogue within Israel evaporated, and with the outbreak of the second intifada, violent fundamentalists began to grow ever more powerful, violent fundamentalists turning themselves into human bombs, endless acts of terrorism in sleepy Jerusalem neighborhoods, in bustling Tel Aviv malls. Bypass roads, walls, separations, checkpoints, bitterness and more bitterness.

As Jews we try to relinquish the makeshift cloak of oppressor which never seemed to fit, then all too often find thrown on us the age-old garment of victim we know so well.

# Peace Unravels

*And God said to Jonah, "Are you so deeply*
*grieved about the plant?" "Yes," he answered,*
*"so deeply that I want to die."*

Downstairs on the kitchen radiator
is yesterday's paper and Lisa says
when the story continues from page one
there is a graphic description
of what the mob did to those two soldiers,
the Israeli Army reservists who got lost in Ramallah.

Downstairs on the kitchen counter
is a plum tart made especially for my Uri
home on a break from his first year at college.
Plum tart is famously his favorite
and it is my pleasure
to make him all his favorites.

Downstairs in the backyard
is our sukkah, the gaily decorated
harvest booth known as *sukkat shlomecha*—
our tabernacle of peace—
and tomorrow I will serve Uri the plum tart
as we all sit together in our tabernacle of peace.

Sukkot is my favorite holiday—
the improbable playhouse that gently
sways in the evening breezes,
the pungent smell of the etrog,
the full-bodied singing of Hallel—
psalms of rejoicing.

Actually, you are not permitted to sit shiva
on a holiday—the holiday interrupts, suspends,
the laws of mourning, the holiday supercedes mourning.
So technically, the mother of a soldier who was thrown
from a window in the town of Ramallah, beaten
to death and paraded through the streets, broken—

that mother, if she follows the Jewish laws,
will not be sitting on a low wooden stool today,
today she can wear leather shoes if she chooses,
she can take a bath, or have sex with her husband,
according to the law.

Yet another move brought us to New England, and once again I was in search of a new venue for tikkun olam. The path of this next journey emerged from the general underbrush of possibilities when I logged onto my e-mail one snowy morning and read a message forwarded to me by my husband. He had come across an announcement on a Web site that Seeds of Peace, an organization I vaguely remembered hearing about through the media, was accepting applications for facilitators to work in their camp for the coming summer. Eddie, thinking of my experience working in Beit Sahur, wondered if this call for applications had my name on it. I printed out the job description and application form, it sat on my desk in the large "current" pile, I read it and reread it and reread it. The job equally frightened me and called to me. I had facilitated those dialogue groups so many years ago, could I face the rage of Palestinians and Israelis again, now? Ultimately, in exactly the way my first rendezvous with dialogue had come over a decade ago, this was a decision that made itself—I felt I had no choice, when the frail hope for peace comes soliciting at your door, the only answer is "Yes."

Seeds of Peace, founded by John Wallach in 1993, is an international organization that runs a summer camp in the woods of Maine for teenagers from the Middle East, South Asia, and other regions of conflict around the world, an opportunity for them to speak honestly together and to find common ground toward realizing a vision of someday living in peace. At camp, the teens are housed in mixed bunks—Palestinians, Afghans, Egyptians, Israelis, Pakistanis, and more, all together. They are offered the pleasures of American camping—swimming, boating, soccer, rock climbing, a wide variety of arts programs—and in addition, every day, sessions of facilitated conflict resolution with the other participants in their particular global region. The delegations of teens are accompanied to camp from their homes all over the world by delegation leaders—adult community leaders and educators from their home communities. My work was with these adult delegation leaders: I co-facilitated dialogue sessions for the Middle East group, and also inaugurated a program of informal writing for all the adult participants, specifically designed to supplement and support the work of dialogue.

I've discovered that a common misconception about the camp and its work is to assume that this is a kind of "preaching to the converted"—that people who would agree to participate must already be "peaceniks." Not so. My first year there found us in the midst of a terrible summer: delegation leaders came with anger and rage and blame directed at the other side, and underneath the anger and rage, the most profound pain I can recall witnessing. No sooner had the polite introductions been completed than the shouting began. Luckily though, they came with more than rage and pain, they came with a common personal courage, the courage it takes to travel to an unknown terrain and have all your assumptions thrown open to question, the courage it takes to be open to the possibility of personal transformation. They shared that courage, they shared a common sense of anguish at the violent and dangerous world they came from, and finally, they shared a desperate longing for peace.

I worked together with a team of facilitators. It was our job to keep everyone in the room, to make a safe space for the stories of delegation leaders to be told and honored. It was our job to model listening, for listening is at the heart of dialogue, listening that makes room for the other, listening out of interest and care, listening with respect, compassion even, being present as your genuine self. Participants in dialogue need to put aside the statistics and propaganda and clever arguments they armed themselves with before they walked in the room—and just listen. And listening is very hard work. As I remarked about myself recently in another context, "I was a good listener for a long time and I am now engaged in a lifelong process of deepening that skill. It's exactly the opposite of riding a bike—*every day, every hour,* you need to *concentrate* yet again to remember how to do it."

185

Some of what they shared with one another were portraits of what seemed at first glance to be mundane reality, like Miryam, a young Palestinianin nurse, who described her day: getting up, going to work, coming home, going to sleep. She hadn't been out of her small community for two years—since the start of the second intifada. At one point she talked about a colleague at her hospital, a young woman from Sweden. Every weekend this colleague takes off for another adventure, up north to the Gallilee, down to a spa on the Dead Sea, swimming in Eilat, exploring the highways and byways of the remarkable beauty of the region; and then of course for longer vacations, she's off to Europe or points East. She comes home with a suntan and stories and says to Miryam, *Why don't you travel on your day off?* And Miryam says to us, *This colleague, with her blond hair and foreign passport, gets a polite, if not flirtatious wave from the soldiers at the checkpoint. I get delay, delay, insult, hostility. I feel myself in a cage—all I can do is get up in the morning, go to work, come home at night and fall into bed. I am like an animal in a cage.*

Sometimes stories emerged in the course of the regional dialogues, sometimes in the plenary group—we had facilitated sessions each day subdivided by region, other daily sessions with all of us together. My friend and colleague Anita, who facilitated the South Asia dialogue for the Indians, Pakistanis, and Afghans, commented to me one day early in our month together that her group, meeting right next door to ours, had halted their session that morning and sat for a time, listening in silence to the screaming that was coming from the Middle East group, unable to continue their own work, so overwhelmed were they by the raw pain under the shouted words.

At other moments in the dialogue, someone would struggle to find his voice to tell about a particular moment, a particular event, and the telling was in so soft a tone that everyone in the room would have to strain to hear, like the story told by Kobi, a young Israeli teacher, about the same age as Miryam. A few weeks before coming to camp, Kobi was called to the morgue to identify a childhood friend, the victim of a terrorist bombing in a Jerusalem café. (The friend's family was out of the country at the time and that made him the closest to the deceased.) He said of course he was nervous—I could see the fear in his body language as he told the story, in fact, he kept clearing his throat, an effort befitting his quiet dignity as he refused to break down and cry. He was led into a room with only a metal gurney, covered by a black sheet, and he was confused because the form under the sheet didn't seem big enough to be a person. When the attendant pulled back the sheet, there was only the charred remains of an arm, with a watch on the wrist. These two friends had recently purchased the same distinctive wristwatch from an Internet catalog, a fancy model to use while snorkeling. That's how he identified his childhood friend.

What did the listeners on both sides hear? That of course is a crucial question when considering what the effects of dialogue are. Perhaps the greatest challenge is to listen to such painful stories and not internalize them as accusations, not respond by becoming defensive, but rather to develop the resources within oneself to reach out with compassion to the person before you. In my experience with dialogue, people move in and out of the capacity for compassion—as in all human relations, sometimes in the heat of an intense moment what you see before you is your enemy, sometimes what you see is a fellow human in pain and your heart is able to open. Yet another possibility is that the stories live inside you, perhaps never to have their effects measured or quantified, working their mystery nonetheless, and a month later or a year later they change how you see "the other" as you meet him in the daily comings and goings of your life back home, that you know now in your bones something you didn't know before, and there's no going back.

Stories might emerge, as above, within the dialogue sessions, at other times they might be shared in one-on-one conversations, as was often the case with Naran, a well-educated professional from Afghanistan, in her late thirties, married with four daughters. Under the Taliban she taught her own

187

children in secret and also held school for other girls. She talked about the absolute necessity for women to be covered at all times, describing how the Taliban would just take girls as they liked, snatch them from the street, never to be seen or heard from again. She described how two of her students, thirteen year olds, quite beautiful, just disappeared one day. The mothers came to her, frantic—had she by chance seen them? No. They were never seen again. Her oldest daughter was too afraid to go out anywhere, even covered—*What if they take me?* When Naran needed to visit family who lived at some distance, not having a car, she would have to go by taxi, but since the Taliban often drove taxis and that was one way girls disappeared, her daughter was too afraid to go out, even in a taxi, even completely covered, even with her mother.

And sometimes stories unfolded as a result of writing prompts I gave participants. (A brief word or two about the logistics of writing with such an international mix: the delegation leaders, like the teens, needed to have an adequate proficiency in English in order to attend camp and participate in dialogue, but by the time I was leading writing at Seeds of Peace I had enough experience to know that people need to be free to write in their first language if they are to make a connection with their own deepest self, and so people were writing in a number of languages—seven, I think, and five different alphabets. Then if they chose to share from what they had written, they could make a running translation of the English, or just tell or talk about the piece.)

I designed writing prompts with a variety of goals, often to provide the opportunity for self-exploration and the comfort that can come from giving words to your pain—it was always understood that writing topics were offered with the option of later sharing or not sharing. Sometimes though my goal was to elicit personal revelations that might echo mutual recognition on less charged (nonpolitical) subjects, like the time I asked them, *Tell a story about yourself when you were sixteen,* the age of some of the teens they each had accompanied to camp. I then might invite participants to share something with the whole group, resulting in special moments of poignancy, surprise, raucous laughter, compassion. At other times after writing, I would divide them in small groups for more intimate sharing opportunities: once when I had sent them off in groups of three to read together (it was the *"when you were sixteen"* writing) one group—all men—an Israeli, a Palestinian, and an Afghan, sat under a tree in intense conversation. When I approached to say the allotted time was over and to suggest they break for lunch, with tender twinkling eyes they invited me to join them, conspiratorially asserting, *We're telling each other secrets.*

Off-campus and evening activities were a rich part of the camp experience. Evenings out might consist of a trip to the local bowling alley, a wonderful excuse for uncontrolled laughter, or an unexpectedly moving visit one morning to the local small town public library, reminding the accompanying Americans not to take for granted the network of institutions that support democracy. Special memories: walking along the rocky Atlantic shore near Portland and the look on Naran's face when she took off her shoes and socks and went wading and then dancing in the cold ocean water... and the evening the camp brought in a pair of fiddlers to accompany and call square dancing, everyone undeniably joyful together for an evening, simply, irrepressibly, joyful.

The international activism that was born for me during that now long ago sabbatical year in Israel continued at my writing desk, then resumed once again at Seeds of Peace. The awareness and empowerment that grew out of the work in Beit Sahur came to permeate everything; now, quite often, quite naturally, I feel called to ask, how can I contribute to creating change. This is, quite simply, a direct outgrowth of the dialogue process, for dialogue is first and foremost about personal transformation, requiring openness to the possibility of transformation, the willingness, the courage, to be open to changing oneself. Interestingly, becoming a change maker has continually effected change in me. But I have not focused solely on the concerns and ongoing work of the Middle East— living in New York, I looked close to home and spent several years working for Beyond Shelter. And then circumstances opened for me to make a contribution in even further corners of the globe—Minsk, Kiev, Moscow.

Predating and simultaneous with the work at Seeds of Peace, I began to join in the mission of Project Kesher, the Chicago-based grassroots organization that supports, trains, and partners with Jewish women leaders across the independent states of the former Soviet Union (FSU). Project Kesher seeks to strengthen and participate in the renaissance of Jewish life occurring throughout the region, helping empower Jewish women to further develop the skills they need to create communities where Judaism, feminism, and democracy can thrive.

Founded in the early 1990s by Sallie Gratch, an American, and Svetlana Yakimenko, a Russian, a dozen years later under the devoted direction of Karyn Gershon, Project Kesher boasts 165 chapters across eight time zones of Russia, Ukraine, Belarus, and Moldova, and is engaged in a truly extraordinary range of programs that are renewing Jewish life, empowering women financially, and securing women's health and safety. What does that mean in more specific terms? Fostering women's study and worship groups, nurturing egalitarian pluralistic religious expression, combating trafficking of young women through legislation and education. Providing materials for ongoing Jewish education for children and adults. Offering computer training programs and seeding micro-enterprise businesses run by women. Developing women's health initiatives (among them activist educational programs to prevent the spread of AIDS). Organizing advocacy, legislation, and education to prevent domestic violence. Supporting a variety of activities in the arts and underwriting women's seders. Reaching out to women and men in other faith traditions to work together on common civic concerns.

190

Who are the women activists and leaders of Project Kesher? Young, old, and middle aged, they come from small cities and towns all across the FSU, places where we in the West have no record even of Jewish communities surviving. Women full of passion to live a Jewish life, hungry to learn about their heritage, women who are activists working for change in their local governments, reaching out to fellow citizens of different ethnicities and faiths to battle the hardships of unemployment and the social ills poverty spawns, moving their communities toward democracy. They are women with complex and rich family legacies, with stories of oppression, of war and revolution and pogrom and dislocation, uncertainty and purge and famine, depression and recession and uncertainty. Women of enormous strength, humor, vitality and curiosity, women committed to family and community, to making change and repairing the world, women who've endured and endure hardships we don't begin to know, commonly living with families in one room, sometimes with two or three generations, with limited hot water, or none at all. Women living out and transmitting Jewish values.

My involvement in Project Kesher, which has brought me several times to teach and speak in Ukraine, in Russia, and in Belarus, initially began as I learned about the organization and its work from an old friend, Marcia Cohn Spiegel. Marty brought her passion and wisdom about community organizing, about Jewish tradition and renewal, to the early years of the organization's development, making numerous trips across Ukraine and Russia, undeterred by her age and the rough conditions she often met on the road. She began involving her friends through fundraising and wound up inspiring me to answer the call for help by beginning to go there myself.

Perhaps not surprisingly, in the weeks leading up to the departure date for my first trip, I had frequent bouts of agonizing self-scrutiny: these women in the FSU who'd been deprived for so long of rich, deep, learned Jewish resources were now going to get—*me*? I don't begin to know enough to be a worthy emissary. All the fears and self-doubt that had characterized my struggles with accepting leadership of the Beit Sahur dialogues resurfaced with a vengeance. But I had by now some years of experience in doing battle with those disempowering inner demons, and somehow in the odd ways fact and circumstance bring us to the important challenges in life, this plane ticket had my name on it.

The purpose of that first trip was to meet with and teach Jewish women activists from across the FSU at an intensive leadership training seminar. I traveled with a group of Jewish women activists from the United States, each bringing to bear her different area of expertise, some leading sessions on community organizing, others on Jewish thought and practice, on women's health, micro-enterprise, group formation, leadership development. My portfolio was spirituality and creativity. Every moment was precious: I used the time allotted to me to read my poetry and to lead writing workshops. Why writing? I reasoned that the way to open a spiritual path was to guide these women in the art of listening—listening to the still, small voice within, and listening then to one another's voices.

I had no idea how culturally alien this process was for them—finding your voice, speaking your truth—and the first writing I asked them to attempt (in Russian of course), *Tell the story of a time when you felt proud of yourself,* provoked an unexpected and fascinating cultural paralysis, and then a tug-of-war. *We can't,* they said. *Try,* I responded. *No,* they resisted. *What's this about?* I inquired. *We've been told all our lives, you are nothing special, you are no different from anyone else, you are all interchangeable. We were commanded, don't be proud of yourself, be proud of the State.* But they were above all, courageous women, so they trusted me and finally wrote and shared, opening for themselves and for each other interior realms full of power and poignancy.

One of those stories: a woman wrote of how a train coming through her small town in the Stalinist era deposited two young children who had been separated from their parents and were being sent home. Except there had been some mix up with the sequence of their train tickets and now, with hundreds of miles to go, they were suddenly without passage, without money, without food. Two waifs on the platform. The woman writing the story said, I couldn't bear it, and so, even in a time when everyone was destitute and suffering, she took up a collection from the people of her community and sent these children onward, to home. Later she got a letter from the parents, full of gratitude beyond words, and the articulation that they (the parents) were incredulous that a Jewish woman would have been capable of such a righteous act of kindness.

Writing was only half of my work with them. In preparation for this trip, I had sent ahead a dozen of my poems to be translated into Russian (almost none of these women knew English and so all of our work there was accomplished with teams of translators). In the last many years, I've used my poetry as a way of making connections, expressing for myself and others the pleasures and sorrows and subtleties of being alive, being Jewish, being a woman. I was understandably concerned though that the cultural gap might be too great to bridge—could my words about my life really speak to the condition of a twenty year old from Moscow, a seventy year old from Minsk, a forty year old from Tula?

In fact, the story of my journey that emerges through the poems—the struggle to overcome poverty, the discovery of Jewish tradition only as an adult, the battle to secure equality as a woman in Judaism, the exploration to uncover my creative gifts and talents and to have faith and pride in myself, the effort to make peace with my family of origin and to learn what I needed to know about making a family of my own, and the journey to becoming an activist who works in collaboration with others to shape a world of social justice—all the stories of my development and growth—are precisely the points of connection I found with the women I met from across the FSU at that first seminar.

193

My poetry resonated deeply with them; they responded to each poem in turn with intense recognition and appreciation. Barely knowing how to say "please" and "good morning" in Russian, I could easily follow line after line of my poems as Luba, the translator, read—I heard where they laughed, I saw where they cried. *Croup,* they cried; *Yizkor,* they laughed, and cried. *My father in his chair* opened a discussion of how we struggle to make meaning at the end of our lives, reflecting on what the process of looking through old photographs is really about and how to help the people we love to do that, how to work through that process. They understood *Lotswife* through the lens of an unrelenting succession of historical traumas they've survived, the tragic stories that are their legacy, and the challenge of making theological sense of it. We discussed the place of women in Jewish life, reflecting on *We All Stood Together,* as they compared the egalitarian models of Project Kesher to what they observed in the Lubovitch emissaries to their communities. And a few nights later, in response to *Healing after a miscarriage,* one woman sought me out to confess the anguish she felt about her abortion—*we all live in one small room, my husband, my son, and I, one small room, my husband without work, it was impossible—another baby, impossible . . . but how I wanted that new life...*

Even I, a poet, had underestimated the power of poetry, the power of naming, to nourish, the power of quietly articulated truths, to sustain. The women took home with them xeroxes of the Russian translations, and over time word got back that in their disparate communities across the FSU the poems were sparking lively and heart-felt interest. Two years passed and then a call came—we want not just a few of the poems, we want all the poems, the stories too—and so I enlisted the help of some friends, Juliet and Phil, Esther and Max, Ruth and Rob, many dear friends from the days in Princeton, and five years after the Vitebsk seminar, we managed to fund the translation and publication of the first edition of this book in Russian.

The publication of the translation occasioned another trip for me to the FSU, this time, an assuredly unique book tour through Ukraine, eighteen days crisscrossing historically rich farmlands, visiting the capitol city of Kiev and three midsize cities of about 350,000 each—Cherkassy, Chernigov and Vinnitsa.

Accompanying me on this journey are Nina Klotsman and Lyubov Zrazhevska. Luba, in her midsixties, the dignified and eloquent chair of her university's department of translation— Luba rendered my book into Russian and for these eighteen days we are all but joined at the hip as she stands by my side translating at the poetry readings and talks I am giving, then translating the responses and questions that follow these presentations, translating the conversations at lunch, breakfast, dinner, translating the driver's random remarks as we crisscross the country, the rabbi's Shabbos morning *drash*, the signs in the supermarket—poor Luba—if I am awake, she is hard at work.

And Nina, in her midforties, originally trained as an architect, now a director of Project Kesher activities in Ukraine— quick intelligence, deep humanity, she is diligent and determined to spread the doing and feeling and being of Jewish to her countrywomen in this vast land, deprived of Jewish possibility for almost a century and now breathless to catch up. When we first met, a mere five years earlier in Vitebsk, Nina seemed painfully shy, now I find myself particularly struck by how she has grown as a leader in competence, confidence, and poise. I see at stop after stop of our journey that she has become a dynamic speaker, a tireless organizer, mentor and leader for the thousands of women she serves. [A year later, at Project Kesher's Voyage on the Volga, Nina *leyns* from the Torah for the first time on Shabbos morning for the assembled congregation of more than two hundred women.]

Though the common perception we as Americans have about Jews and Jewish life in the FSU is that the Jews who remain there are an old, dying generation that requires our support for basic needs and which in another ten years or so will be only a memory, the next weeks of this journey dispel any such myths. I meet women and men—in synagogues, in intimate study groups, at big city community centers, in Rosh

195

Hodesh groups, in interfaith and cross-cultural civic meetings, in computer training classes, in Jewish dance troupes—whose thoughtfulness, vitality, Jewish curiosity and commitment, human and spiritual depth, exactly mirror the best of the women and men I know here in America. Again and again I meet with groups that look demographically like replications of our own Jewish communities, vibrant citizens in their twenties, thirties, forties, fifties, sixties, and onward.

One balmy night in Chernigov, I offer a few of my poems for study and discussion to forty women gathered for their monthly Rosh Hodesh group, one of the city's three well-established Project Kesher groups, this one known as "the Irinas" because by coincidence so many of the founding members were named Irina. Most of the women are in their thirties, many coming from a day of work, with a quick stop at home to feed children and husbands. The room quickly fills with warm laughter and deep sharing. At one point they begin to talk about the high rate of unemployment, the deep poverty that brings suffering and shame. We reflect on how to stay connected to friends and community in hard economic times and they underscore the importance of this group in their lives, allowing them to come together for social and spiritual nourishment on common neutral turf. As the evening ends, I am invited to a rehearsal the next night of a Jewish dance troupe that a number of them participate in. I accept, and the following evening yet another extraordinary experience unfolds, as Israeli melodies fill the air and the lithe bodies of these Jewish women explode with joy.

At Solomon University (the Brandeis of Kiev) I read poems that reflect the stages of spiritual development with a special focus on women's experience. The undergraduates and graduate students listen in such rapt attention that they open the deepest places in my heart. When I read *The first time we made Shabbos together,* a poem about falling in love, they understand it is about falling in love with a life's partner-to-be, and also about falling in love with Shabbat, and also about falling in love with the beauty and pleasure of living as a Jewish woman.

196

One young doctoral candidate in philosophy with luminescent dark eyes declares solemnly at the end, "There was another presence in this room with us today as we shared our souls with each other. God was here in this room today." Stalin is turning over in his grave.

The next day, on a walking tour of Kiev, I see families begging on the street, a mother sitting on the sidewalk with a baby at her breast and her hand out imploring passersby. The economy seems to be at a standstill, and poverty and a high rate of unemployment affect every aspect of life. There is no real middle class—just a tiny minority of the privileged and the vast majority who struggle to put food on the table. Anyone who has the tiniest bit of soil here grows vegetables, raises a few chickens for eggs, uses these provisions for their own sustenance and then comes to market to see what they can sell for additional income.

When meeting someone new, I quickly learn not to ask the standard American question, "What do you do?" as an entry to further conversation because hardly anyone actually "does" what they are trained to do—people are happy to have any kind of job that puts food on the table. Thus, as Nina remarks, "The computer centers created in partnership by Project Kesher and ORT (there are currently fifteen centers across the FSU) provide women—Jewish and non-Jewish—with technical training and the promise and reality of helping to support their families. This occupational training can alleviate the economic hardships that often trigger domestic violence, can give a battered woman the means to leave an abusive relationship, and can also serve to prevent the trafficking of women—when they can get real work that pays decently, young girls are far less vulnerable to getting caught up in shady schemes to 'earn good money abroad,' offers that turn out to be slave labor prostitution rings with no way out and no way home." (All of Project Kesher's vocational training and social action initiatives purposely include women and men of other religions and ethnic groups, consciously building the bridges and alliances that combat anti-Semitism.)

In every city, I offer a program for the local Hesed, the community centers supported by the Joint Distribution Committee where the Jewish elderly gather each day for a hearty lunch, companionship, intellectual stimulation, medical care, educational and arts programs. (The JDC does magnificent work, over and over I was impressed by their devotion and their efficiency.) At the Hesed in Vinnitsa, one poem I read— *My Friends Baked Cake and We Ordered Lox and Whitefish from the Deli,* a poem that whimsically describes a nervous new mother at the bris of her son—sparks some incredible sharing. While in America, where circumcision is common in the general population, the poem always draws knowing, appreciative laughs, in Vinnitsa it opens a conversation about the long history of persecution in this part of the world and how a family would have placed their son in mortal danger by circumcising him. They tell me only now again do some parents circumcise their sons, and even now it is seen as an act of courage and faith in the future. I wonder how this historical relationship to circumcision has affected their understanding of themselves as Jews; my privilege as an American feels boundless to me.

Back in Kiev, I spend an afternoon with eighteen-year-old Vika, one of the Solomon University undergraduates. She tells me about her life and family, including stories of her grandfather who lied about his age to go fight the Fascists in World War II and defend the Motherland Ukraine. She takes me to Babi Yar, the ravine outside Kiev where in September 1941, close to 34,000 Jews were marched and then machine-gunned, describing how the mass of people, disproportionately women and children, were forced to stand four deep so that one bullet could claim four victims. Each city, each town I will visit has its own Babi Yar: in Tulchin my "tour guide" was Rita, almost seventy. Rita spent age five to nine there in a concentration camp, Death's Noose. What she described to me was indescribable, leaving me numb, shaken, hollow. Yet every day this trip offers powerful reaffirmation—of mystery, of miracle, of how this people have survived as Jews, refusing to die, refusing to be blotted out, and now, once again full of vitality, once again curious, open and eager to celebrate their Jewish heritage.

Stark against the background of Babi Yar's unholy land-
scape that Vika and I circle together, her innocence and hun-
ger to know everything about me, my writing, my Jewish life,
my husband, my children, are moving, pure. She is overflow-
ing with energy and hope for the future, eager to talk with me
about how women can creatively mediate the relationship
between tradition and modernity, how women can make
changes in Jewish life and ritual, adding our own contribu-
tions, how women can make changes that fully include us and
thus strengthen and enhance the power and beauty of what we
have all inherited. Vika is feisty, curious, strong-willed; I find
myself fantasizing her as a daughter-in-law.

In Chernigov, a city whose exquisite, numerous churches
go back to the thirteenth century, five of us sitting at breakfast
one morning begin to talk about the Holocaust. I finally allow
myself to voice a question that kept me awake most of the night
before and wonder out loud how they can pass the central
square every day and not think back to the day in November
1941, when all the Jews were herded into that square, then
marched to the outskirts of town and shot. The theatre director
at the table declares with passion, "I love my city," and then they
share with me the complex layers of their relationships to non-
Jews: all but one of them has some Ukrainian grandparents;
several speak of the heroic Ukrainians who hid or otherwise
saved the lives of their mothers, grandmothers, young cousins
during World War II; they tell how their fathers and grandfa-
thers fought to defend Ukraine in that war; and finally, some
are themselves married to Ukrainian men. Like many of their
American sisters on the other side of the ocean, they too have
identities with permeable boundaries, a fluid sense of ancestry
and family.

Cherkassy, Shabbos afternoon, a presentation of my book
to the City library. Gathered are twenty women, mostly not Jew-
ish, each representing her own religious or ethnic community
in the city, or one of the numerous civic organizations. They
each have been invited either because they already are impor-
tant partners in Project Kesher's work, or because this event will

hopefully be the beginning of future collaboration with Project Kesher. I am amazed and gratified by their whole-hearted responsiveness to the poems I read and we share on a variety of substantial issues raised by the book. An intense conversation develops about the upbringing of boys and girls, and one woman remarks, "My son is my most sensitive child, but I must teach him that boys don't cry." Later, she is the one who initiates a discussion about men who are violent, who can't express their pain in words, and instead lash out with fists and guns. Throughout the afternoon I am aware of Nina making careful mental notes of which issues to pursue further with whom, and of how to leverage this "literary" conversation into future activism.

In Vinnitsa, at an event sponsored by the Jewish Agency, I speak to a standing room only crowd about the work I've done facilitating dialogue with Israelis and Palestinians in Israel. Together we share our heartache at "the situation." After years of facing American audiences on this subject, I have slowly learned to be a respectful and sensitive listener. Half the audience tonight demonize Palestinians and are hostile to any hint that peace with *them* is possible, the other half are adamant that it is necessary and urgent to pursue peace whether it seems possible or not. Passions run high, I am of course used to tension when I address this subject, but I cannot recall ever having been so forcefully challenged by an audience anywhere. Afterward they surprise me with a late night feast that has been prepared in my honor; with twenty people around the table, they manage to stretch the bottle of schnapps to last for many rounds of toasts— to Israel! to peace! to the children! to Shabbos! to poetry and poets! Again, as with other sessions on this trip, other published poets are in the room, this time one who asks if I know the work of Yehuda Amichai and is overwhelmed to hear I met him on several occasions: this poet from Ukraine who an hour earlier had asked me the hardest question of the evening, now sits across from me with soft eyes and an open heart. Impossible not to fall in love with the passion, the purity, the soulful depth of these people.

Kabbalat Shabbat with the Rosh Hodesh group in Vinnetsa. After we *daven*, they want to hear about my life as a Jewish woman. I share the long ago joy of my young adult Jewish discovery and then the struggle to make an equal place for women at the banquet of ancient Jewish ritual and practice. They know just what joys I am referring to, though they smile at "the struggles" and say, "We are lucky, our men don't mind sharing these things!" Onto the program, an explication of my poem *Lotswife*, an uncovering of this troubled, unholy biblical family, the family violence hidden between the lines, and the eventual promise of redemption embedded in the story. They have participated along with eighty other groups across the FSU in Project Kesher's program "Sixteen Days to End Domestic Violence," they are appreciative as the ancient story and the contemporary poem speak so profoundly to current realities, appreciative to sit and study together with a woman. It is not a novelty for them though—their rabbi, Iyara Solovy, with whom I spent Wednesday and Thursday, is also a woman.

Iyara, Nina, Luba, and I are driving through the lush green Ukrainian countryside toward the small town of Bratslav where Iyara spent her early childhood in her grandparents' home. She tells me stories of Rebbe Nahman, the eighteenth-century Hasidic master who lived and taught here and made Bratslav famous. She also tells me stories of her grandfather, a Bratslaver *hasid* and leader of this small (then underground) Jewish community until his death in the early 1990s. Iyara herself, at twenty-nine, has just completed an intensive two-year program at Machon, the World Union of Progressive Judaism's Institute for Jewish Studies in Moscow, which accepts native-born students and trains them to become para-rabbis who go back to their communities to serve as teachers and spiritual leaders. Like some of the others who have just graduated with her, and some who've gone before, she hopes to continue her studies and receive full rabbinic ordination. When I ask Iyara whether she thinks her grandfather would approve of her serving as a rabbi, she breaks into a radiant smile and responds, "He was progressive, and he loved me very much. Besides," she adds, "you know, Hasidim in their time were reformists."

A side trip to Kazatin to visit Natasha Slobodyanik, a multitalented woman not yet thirty, stunning, funny, vivacious, a dancer, a teacher, a facilitator, and gifted group leader, mother of a young daughter, owner of her own small business, soon heading for a leadership position in Project Kesher's Moscow office. In 1998, when I met her first in Vitebsk, she was not yet twenty-four and had already been the driving force behind a coalition of women's groups that elected seven women to public office in her home town of Kazatin. Her energy, her passion for life and for all things Jewish are contagious. She has arranged a sumptuous meal for us at a wonderful local restaurant and in the course of the lunch, initiates a conversation with me about how organizing in major cities differs from the work she's done previously in smaller venues. Because she solicits my thoughts on the matter, I share what I've observed, but leave feeling, as always, she's light-years ahead of me.

The final Sunday morning, a long drive northward back to Borispol, to the airport. Our driver of these last days, with whom I've made a soulful connection, gives me a gift of his favorite music tape, mostly vintage Louis Armstrong and some Frank Sinatra. I reciprocate with a tape that includes Bob Dylan. With rich farmlands, cows, goats, chickens, and horse-drawn buggies disappearing behind me in a blur, I hear the harmonica and that familiar twang, *"How many roads must a man walk down . . ."* *". . . and the times they are a-changin',"* and suddenly I realize that the vitality, the energy, the life force I have felt every day here—the green shoots of being Jewish that we had no reason to expect or hope for in this part of the world ever again—are echoes of another time and place of unexpected rebirth, and I feel blessed to have been a witness to this holiness and hope being born once again.

# 9

*Daily Prayer*

Over the years I have slowly come to see the need to mediate, to integrate, how I live in the world as an activist, focused on large and complex moral and ethical issues, and how I live day by day, noticing the minutia of life, living in the moment and so being spiritually nourished and enlivened. As I look back on the unspoken assumptions of my upbringing, I see that I was acculturated as a child of the fifties—more precisely, a *girl* of the fifties—raised to care for the small circle of my immediate family, the husband and children I was supposed to have. What my years of political involvement have taught me is that being a full human being necessitates looking past that small tight nuclear circle to find my place in the larger world, and also necessitates taking time for myself, my needs and development as an individual. In other words, I needed to both widen the focus of my attention and narrow the focus of my attention. Making room for both, moving awareness back and forth between the small and the large— that's the dance.

More and more I see the profound value of attention to and respect for the fabric of everyday life—what are the ordinary tasks and what are the ordinary objects that take up my time and go to make up my day. The reality that I have had deep and earnest and ongoing conversations with a musician from Kabul, a physicist from Bombay, an educator from Cairo, a playwright from Chernigov, cannot distract me from listening closely to a newly arrived and perhaps lonely academic in my little New England town, to the director of the local crisis center who comes to share her writing practice with me, to the neighbor on my street who has just lost her younger brother to cancer, to the woman behind the supermarket counter from whom I buy my fish. I need to be grounded in that place where I plant tulips in the autumn and shovel snow in the winter, where I drive to the local high school that is the site of my voting precinct and where I cast ballots for town mayor, state senator, and president of the United States. If at one time perhaps I took these activities and encounters for granted, I now see them as uniquely important. Dramatic moments of meeting in distant lands occur unpredictably, occasions for celebration are few and far between, crises come and go. In fact, life is largely made up of a warp and woof of ordinary moments, casual encounters, subtle opportunities. If I am to be fully alive, then I must be alive in those moments and with those people. I must learn to stop and look and really see, to listen, to hear, to hold, to finger, to contemplate, to take care with the minutia of my life, the seemingly "ordinary" moments and artifacts that are so easy to miss. It's a spiritual reinvention of the wheel—traditional Judaism with its blessings for fruit, bread, rainbows, twilight, a beautiful woman, the king as he passes in procession—all were attempts to wake us up to the moment, the now, the myriad forms of life as it pulsates around and within us.

# Supermarket Prayer

Last week in the supermarket
at an unlikely hour
I saw a woman I know.
She tried to avoid me,
pretended not to remember me,
but I had unwittingly trapped her,
blocked escape in the tuna fish aisle.

I just wanted to say hello,
my cruelty was inadvertent,
but up close I saw
her hair was in disarray
and dirty, her face
without its careful mask
of lipstick, blusher, shadow.
She was wearing a ratty old jacket,
the discard of her husband
or perhaps her teenaged son.
Nine thirty, on a Tuesday morning,
dressed like that—
suddenly I knew she was out of work
and ashamed. And coming undone
there in the tuna fish aisle.

I tried as best I could
to help her cover her nakedness
but all that day and the next
she haunted me.
How strange, I thought,
how strange and how sad
that she should feel threatened, judged,
shamed by me.

The rabbis say
when you bring color to someone's face
it's as if you shed their blood.
Forgive me.
May you be restored to your full self
soon, speedily, in our day.
And let us say amen.

A Project Kesher group in Belarus used this poem as an opportunity to explore the meaning of the title, *Supermarket Prayer*—what constitutes a prayer? Was something a legitimate prayer only if it was found in an (old) prayerbook? Who wrote the poems in our prayerbook(s) and what did those prayer-makers have in common? I was fascinated to hear them delineate the criteria: the group, mostly women, said the authors of our printed prayers were Jewish, were men, and believed in God. And then I nudged the conversation a little further— were all prayers necessarily declarations of faith? What are the varieties of religious experience that might impel a prayer? Wonderful to tell them of new prayers, wonderful to see as we talked how the women in the room came closer and closer to entertaining the possibility that prayermakers could be people not so different from themselves—doubters, seekers, believers, full of joy, confusion, thanksgiving, anger, awe.

A consideration of the same poem in a Project Kesher women's group one June night in Ukraine a few years later elicited a quiet sharing of the pain and shame of unemployment; how we struggle as individuals to be a healing presence, pursuers of tikkun olam. One woman in particular spoke of a friend, struggling with poverty and hunger. She posed to the group the difficult question, how can I help her—she won't even come to eat in my house because she cannot return such an invitation. Around the circle the women grappled with this delicate quandary, agreeing that sometimes it is possible to offer concrete assistance, sometimes it is not possible, but it is always possible to offer the kindness of friendship and respect. They concluded finally that this was one reason the group was so vital for them: we can come here to this community center, gather together and enjoy the warmth of each other's company and some wonderful food without incurring an obligation to reciprocate, an obligation that many of us could not easily meet.

In America, how have audiences responded to this poem? Sometimes by observing how hard it can be, to be together, simply, honestly, in our common humanity, to acknowledge that sometimes I have been the shopper who unwittingly causes pain, and sometimes I have been the woman down on her luck and ashamed, how hard to acknowledge, I have been both. We struggle for our dignity, our fragile dignity. And just beneath the surfaces we hurry past are layers of meaning, sometimes profound, sometimes whimsical, sometimes an amalgam of both.

From commonplace venues to unseen apparel, it adds an entirely new dimension to our lives to take notice of the "ordinary," ordinary scenes, ordinary objects.

# Underwear

There are two kinds of people in the world—
people who spend money on their underwear
and people who don't.
I know a lot about people who don't.

They're older.
They've been married a long time
and expect to remain so.
(They're married to other people

whose underwear is also dingy,
torn, stretched out.) Or,
they've been alone a long time
and expect to remain so.

They've also stopped buying new sheets
for their beds. They're not expecting
to meet anyone new in the bedroom
so they're not worried about making a good impression.

They don't spend much money on clothes at all.
They don't have much money,
and if they did, underwear would still
be a low priority.

They have trouble treating themselves well—
they have to work at it very hard
and don't often succeed.
They pass underwear displays in department stores,

sometimes stop to check the price tags,
and make a mental note that if someday
they ever have a lot of money
they'll buy several sets in several colors.

They don't ever expect to have a lot of money.
They know the expensive underwear
in lots of colors wasn't made for them,
but there's so much of it, someone must buy it.

They're very curious
about the people who do.
I don't know anything about those people—
you'll have to ask someone else.

Because I've hardly ever worked in a real office, and most often have freelanced my skills as an editor, a writer, a political organizer, a teacher, I've never had office paraphanelia—the fancy briefcase, the Rolodex. I've found it more convenient over the years when struggling to keep track of a multitude of friends and professional contacts to use a succession of small, portable address books.

When I was young and starting out, I never imagined the emotional weight that might accrue from this particular habit.

# Moving ahead moving on moving along moving

The cover of my old address book
fell off, the pages are tearing.
I bought the new book this morning—
small, brown, fake leather cover,
Woolworth's.

I think that's the problem:
if I bought a really good one
it would last forever
and I wouldn't have to redo it
every couple of years,
but since it's something only for me,
something no one else sees
(sort of like my underwear)
I'm cheap about it.

People move so often nowadays
I really should do the whole thing
in pencil, just keep erasing.
That's not the real problem though,
the problem is, what to do with the people.

Sometimes there are dead people
in my old worn-out address book.
I can't write them into the new one of course,
but it hurts to leave them behind
yet another time.

There are distant relatives,
people I haven't seen in years,
and I transfer them
from book to book to book.
I have no intention of contacting them,

but my mother would be disappointed
if she knew I had omitted them
on purpose.

Here's a family that settled in Israel
more than a year ago,
they never sent me their new address.
In my old book
they still live in Los Angeles
and we're still friends.

There's a man I liked a lot,
met him in a T-group.
I just have the phone number, no address.
It's hard to let go of people
who've seen you without a mask.
If I recopy the number
maybe sometime I will call.

Here's a boy I thought I loved
in 1967. We lost touch
and when he turned up again
he was "religious"
with a wife and three kids.
We kept promising to get together
but I couldn't bear to see him
with a wife in a wig and three toddlers
in a dingy Bronx apartment.
They left the country years ago
but I keep recopying his name
(and hers—the wife I never met)
with an address in the Bronx.
Really, in my mind's eye,
he's still a Harvard undergraduate.

There are the requisite number
of divorces with arrows to show
they've gone their separate ways.
Once I recopy them it will look as if

they were never
together.

Sometimes I remember to pencil in
a new baby
otherwise I tend to forget—
the name
the sex
the fact of existence.

You probably think I'm crazy
but I save
all my tattered
fake leather
Woolworth
address books.
They're in the top center drawer
of my dresser.

When my play *Across the Jordan* was selected for inclusion in an anthology of Jewish women playwrights, I was asked by the editor to write an accompanying autobiographical essay. While I later was required to trim some details, in the first draft of that essay I gratefully acknowledged some of the teachers who had added a richness of spirit to my young life. Did Mel Petigrow understand what a balm his simple kindness was to me in junior high school? Would Samuel Gallant have thought I'd remember his moral passion three decades after he assigned us *Johnnie Got His Gun,* a chilling antiwar novel, and the powerful novel of social protest, *The Last Angry Man?* Fond memories of Dominick Bongiorno, infecting eleventh and twelfth graders with an excitement in Shakespeare so great it could not be contained. And Vera Lachmann, who fled Germany in 1939, who would sit cross-legged on the desk in the front of the classroom, her wiry gray hair knotted in a compact bun, her dark Old Country dresses reminiscent of my grandmother's; cross-legged, sitting on the desk, she read to us from *The Bacchae,* reflecting on the arrogant purity of Hippolytus, cross-legged, sitting on the desk, she introduced me to Thomas Mann's *The Magic Mountain.* The fire of her words is within me still.

When we are impressionable and powerless, a teacher can hold great sway for good or for evil. Teachers easily capture our attention, seize our imagination. We observe their every quirk, their every nuance. Their words and their idiosyncracies are food for thought. And those moments when they touched you live on into eternity. But not all the teachers and all the moments of touching are holy.

# Choice

Mr. Greenberg in the sixth grade,
a mean-spirited bald man
who turned red when he yelled at us,
not beet-red—not that red—
but blood-red,
was a man who had no business
spending so much time with children,
having power over young children.

He gave us a choice always
when we didn't get the homework right—
"Are you stupid or lazy?"

I always hated that, never forgot that,
I hated it most of all,
even more than I hated the way
he tried to destroy Paul Hecht who
just wanted to sit in the back
and read, and believe me,
I hated him a lot for Paul Hecht,
but even more I hated him
for stupid or lazy.

It seemed evil to offer a choice
which wasn't a choice,
to pretend to be offering a choice,
to force you to make a choice,
when you knew you had no choice.

In my experience over the years with the death of various family members and friends, I observe that after a person dies it can take sometimes vastly diffferent amounts of time for the reality of a particular death to be absorbed. First and most stark for me was with my mother. I calculate it took me about seven years to acknowledge in my heart that she was really gone, wasn't off on some too-long vacation, wouldn't ever be coming back.

Similar though not so extreme was my reaction to the death of friends Ira Silverman and Hannah Ticktin. Though both had been ill for a long time, both died quite young and both were so vibrant in life, so passionate and fully present, it was impossible to comprehend that they were gone.

Hershel Matt, a wonderful rabbi and a warm and gentle soul with whom I spent many festive holiday celebrations and with whom I occasionally shared philosophical and religious conversation, was the only person I think I've ever known who professed to believe in life after death. He died quite suddenly of a heart attack on a Shabbos afternoon. Returning home after his funeral, I sat up that evening missing his conversation, his earnest manner, his shy sly gentle smile and I wondered literally, where is Hershel.

# First night in the grave

*for Hershel*


It's cold the first night in the grave,
the snow falling,
the body just starting to understand.

The snow is falling
and the spirit wanders
back and forth
from here to there,
just starting to understand.

I want to translate this poem into German,
a solemn language,
a language I don't understand.
I think it will be a small comfort to me
in a language I don't understand.

I am missing you tonight
with the snow falling,
your first night in the grave.

It's a mitzvah (literally, "commanded by God," though in common parlance, tellingly, it's come to mean something less demanding—"a good deed") to comfort the mourner. This might entail attending the funeral, writing a condolance note, paying a shiva call—a visit to the house of mourning during the seven days after the burial.

It's not easy to be present for someone in pain. While there is an elaborate, graceful etiquette prescribed by the tradition for paying a shiva call, most moderns are unaware of any such age-old guideline to wisdom. Often people enter a house of mourning full of the news of the day, gossip, the latest political bruhaha: they chattter on relentlessly, hard at work pretending nothing is amiss. These visitors are from the school of thought that says the best approach is to offer cheerful distraction to the bereaved, creating an atmosphere not unlike that of a cocktail party. Then there is the ever popular visitor to the house of mourning who seizes the opportunity to unload her sadness, her problems, her experience with loss; also in this category are those who regale the mourner with gruesome tales of persons they know or have heard of who've suffered even greater losses.

What is appropriate behavior paying a shiva call? Right up front, succinctly tell your friend how sorry you are. So simple, seemingly too obvious to even mention, but actually hard to do, hard because "I'm sorry" feels so inadequate. In fact though, those modest words are a great comfort. Then, if you knew the deceased, share some stories or remembrances. Even better, be quiet and allow the mourner to take the lead. Perhaps best of all, if you didn't know the person, simply ask, "Could you tell me about your sister?" And then, most important, sit and listen.

But as anyone who himself has been in mourning knows, the days of shiva are just the beginning of a long period of sorrow, often many months of waking in the morning, innocently coming to consciousness, only to be knocked down again as the reality hits—I'm in this world without her, she's gone.

221

After the eulogies, after the shiva, you go to visit your friend again. There's not much you can say, it's your presence that says it, your presence says, "You are not utterly abandoned." And after each visit, when you leave, you quietly take a little of their pain away with you.

Then the time comes when you want to help your friend reenter the world. How do you help someone you love to let go of his pain, to remember peace, pleasure, again?

# Words of Comfort

The sky is still blue,
she's dead and the sky is still blue:
How stupid of me to offer comfort
with words like "the sky is still blue,
look at the blue of the sky"—

I'd forgotten what an outrage it is
that the sky is still blue—
the insistence of the sky—still blue,
the indifference of the sky—still blue,
the sky is no comfort to you—still blue.

But I also said,
"Look into your son's eyes
and remember why you love him."

And I said,
"Eat some watermelon
and taste its sweet juice."

The watermelon of course is like the sky
but I won't yield the point of your son's eyes—
look into your son's eyes
and remember why you love him.

My earliest ideas about snow, as well as about many other things, came from my mother's mother who lived across the street from us when I was growing up and who we saw every day—she was the surrogate mother while our mother was at work. When we were little, my brother Roger and I would beg Grandma, "Tell us a story, tell us a story about the Old Country, when you were a little girl." Our favorite story was about snow.

When Grandma was five, six, seven, her mother taught her at home. Then when she got a bit older, she was sent to the nearest big town with a real school. In the daytime she learned reading, writing; then after school, on weekdays, she boarded with a family in town and as payment helped with their cleaning and cooking. On occasional weekends she hitched a ride from a passing wagon or took the long walk home. One Friday in December, an early snow began to fall, but Bertha was filled with a longing to see her mother. She began to walk. She walked and walked and was tired and so cold and she wanted for just a few minutes to lie down and rest in the snow but she knew if she did she would die there. So Bertha kept on walking. The darkness came, still she walked. Finally the little house was in sight. Her mother, looking from the window, saw her and ran out of the house, calling "Bertha! Bertha!" scooped her up and carried her inside to warm arms, blankets, food and drink.

The story told me: when my grandmother was little, she was loved. My grandmother, even then, was brave and determined. Though it looks pretty, snow is dangerous.

# winter            wonderland

relentless

                silent                        white death

        falling

                        from

            the sky

    fills                        my body            and soul

                with        such

                            dread

    I    cannot

                catch

        my        breath.

                        This        time        I'm    safe

but        maybe                        out                        there

        someone        I        love

                                                isn't.

A postscript: the first time I traveled with Project Kesher to the FSU, I was headed for a leadership training seminar being held in Vitebsk. In the months before departure, I kept studying maps of the region, my eyes continually straying from Belarus to Slovakia where all of my mother's family had once lived, including her father Maurice and her mother, my Grandma Bertha. I could see that Belarus and Slovakia weren't so very close, but surely Vitebsk was closer than I had ever been and might ever again be to the towns of my grandparents, my great grandparents. And finally I allowed myself to use this opportunity to make an ancestral pilgrimage.

A few days after leaving Vitebsk, I was on a bridge in Slovakia overlooking the town of Martense where Bertha had lived, where the little house in the "snow story" had once stood. Not much left of Martense to see, but Eddie and I spent the next few days in Zilina, described by my grandmother as "the next big town with a real school," Zilina, also the ancestral home of Maurice, Bertha's husband, my grandfather. Zilina turned out to be more than a town, rather a beautiful city dating back to the Middle Ages and where I was able to trace my grandfather's family to the beginning of the nineteenth century, if not earlier still. It was one of the most profound gifts of my life to stand at the graves of my great-grandparents and my great-great-grandparents—the first family member to visit those graves since World War II when all the cousins, aunts, and uncles who had not emigrated were killed by the Nazis. In the regional archive, Eddie and I found numerous records of family births, marriages, and deaths and intriguing unexpected details about family members who had lived in the nineteenth century. We discovered the site of my great grandparents' home and sat in a grotto restaurant which had once been the basement of their house. And the last morning there, I walked along the country road that linked Martense and Zilina, walked on that road where my grandmother once walked as a little girl, and where, one snowy night in December, more than a century ago, she had almost succumbed to the cold and the snow.

In the years growing up we kept all our photographs in shoeboxes. Several times a year (often I think in inclement weather, during bouts of cabin fever) I would prevail on my mother, take out the photographs, let's look at the photographs. I could spend many minutes studying a particular picture, not unlike the way I stand before the portraits of Rembrandt or Vermeer, with an intensity and a need to know, a need to understand, which penetrates the face, the pose, the eyes, the tilt of the head, which struggles to penetrate the soul: Who is this? What is her story? My mother was insistent that staring at people was rude, but this rule seemed not to apply to inert faces.

As a child, I loved best the precious picture we had from Europe of my maternal great-grandparents, seated regally, imperiously, flanked from behind by their five adult children (this photograph most of all, had inspired my need to journey to Zilina); the photo of my grandmother and her sister as young new immigrants, starkly dressed in mourning for their mother, unable to hide from the camera the pain of their early loss; shots of my mother, my father, and my aunt enjoying a day at the beach in 1920s swimsuits, the long hair of the women whipped by a strong wind: in this series of pictures the three of them are convulsed in laughter, and so somehow these pictures never failed to induce uncontrollable fits of laughter in us children.

Now I am again a detective, scrutinizing snapshots of my own childhood, studying the pictures of myself and my brothers for clues, for solutions to mysteries with fewer and fewer surviving witnesses. How do we stand with each other, with our parents, what transpired between one year's photographic record and the next? How do we look at each other or not look at each other and who was likely to have stood behind the camera that time to account for such an expression on the subject's face?

A few years back, the daughter of dear friends was celebrating her bat mitzvah and I determined to write a poem in her honor. As I scanned in my mind the many memories of this girl I had known from birth, I curiously kept coming back to a photograph I had taken once of her with Lisa when they were little girls together. Something in that early photograph captured for me the spirit of this child.

# The Photograph

*for Tamara*


There you are in the photograph
a delicate girl of three or four—
your chin is tilted, your face at an incline
waiting to receive the kiss.

May you always be so—
receptive and trusting, open to love,
and may the world receive you
again and again as in the photograph
rewarding your faith with kisses.

When I was about nine, Margaret who lived across the street and was seven months younger but always two steps ahead of me, asked in that superior tone she sometimes took if I knew what menstruation was. Making a valiant effort to avoid the humiliation of being one-upped yet again, and figuring that prefixes must be there for a reason, I ventured, "I don't exactly remember but I know it has something to do with men." Margaret, triumphant, "Go ask your mother!"

It's curious given how much of our lives as women we spend menstruating, that aside from the occasional jokes or gripes about cramps or PMS, how little we talk with each other about this cycle of blood. The terror with which we sometimes wait to see the red spot on the toilet paper, the anguish when we prayed not to see it but there it was. The bother of it, the power of it, ultimately the loss of it.

# Me di t a ti on   o n   Men s tru a tion

I'm not feeling it a blessing to be a woman
in her prime      the cells inside me rioting
about to explode      black moods
depression rage    the aching
the waiting      a victim
brought    low
that's
me

Do I ever rejoice in how I am made?
Yes   with a baby at my breast
and      in      lovemaking
alive with pleasure
throbbing glowing
triumphant
free

But   then   again   this   monthly   assault
the    undertoe,    the    tide that    pulls
mercilessly dashing me against the rocks
this  pounding of rage,      overwhelming
overpowering          poor  cowering   me
How      shall I  not     curse    the    tide
as it            pulls    my soul     at will?

A prayer:
some day, some month
perhaps    this      month
let my   body and   its blood
at long last   teach me the lesson
I struggle so  against  accepting—
let go    let go    let go   give up   control
surrender    to the    flow  of  life     within.

As the time for her becoming a bat mitzvah approached, my daughter expressed great excitement at the thought of beginning to light candles on Friday night as I did. I knew that in many traditional homes (particularly Lubovitch, which even puts ads in the Friday *New York Times* informing "Jewish women and girls" what the proper hour is for candlelighting each week) it is the custom for girls to light not the adult complement of two candles but rather to light one. And so I wondered, should I give Lisa one to light? Should I give her two to light? If she started out by lighting one, when would she graduate to two? When she leaves for college, moving out to live on her own (something Lubovitch girls do not do)? When she gets married? What if she doesn't get married? Are single Lubovitch women forever relegated to one candle? While it was easy at this point in my internal argument to decide that Lisa would start with two candles, the whole question got me to thinking . . .

In the early sixties when I was becoming a teenager, the ethos was still quite strong that the less defined a girl was in her taste, her preferences, her desires, her identity, the more easily she'd find herself a husband. (I think young women of today don't really believe that that's why lots of their mothers were sent to college. The world has changed that much.) The reasoning went something like this: it's the woman's role to be flexible, compatible, and so the less committed you are to habits and paths of your own, the more natural you will find it to cleave to the habits and paths of your husband.

But what if your particular life story turns out not to have a husband in the script? It seems an impossible contradiction to me to forge ahead and build a full life while simultaneously saving a place at the table. How can a woman move toward inner peace with such inherent inner contradictions?

# I commit myself

The years slip by,
new moon, full moon.

I skid on the ice,
wait for summer—

here it is—
then gone.

I don't get to the beach
as often as I think I will.

These past few summers
I don't even have time for a tan,

then winter again,
and ice.


I commit myself to a life,
a specificity.

I set up a home,
start buying my own china.

I'm liberated,
strong and proud,

refuse to live out my days
in the waiting room.

But I had hoped
there would be more.

Once on a flight returning home from a week in Paris, I had five hours of soulful conversation with a French seatmate. (Another time, landing in Newark after a flight from Florida, I heard the person sitting next to me exclaim, "You haven't once lifted that pen from your paper since we took off!") So talking to strangers while in transit is not usual for me. Even more than writing, or reading, I enjoy the luxury when traveling solo of just daydreaming.

But, who knows why, we got to talking, this Frenchman and I. We talked a lot about God (perhaps in fact that's why we got to talking—my French is good enough for the cover of the magazine he was reading to have caught my eye—big bold cover story, "Where is God today?") We talked about having daughters in their senior year of high school, about the merits and shortcomings of a number of American universities. Though I was thoroughly enjoying his conversation and his company, at one point in the brief hiatus airlines impose on transAtlantic flights between the serving of dinner and the serving of breakfast, I excused myself saying I needed to be quiet for a while, I was trying to think about my life. Later when we got to talking again, I asked him how often he thought about his life. With a quiet earnestness that contradicted the stereotype of the high-powered corporate executive, he replied, "Every day." I was impressed.

# Over There

Sometimes
out of the corner
of my eye
I get a glimpse
of my life.

In a flash
in a moment—
over there—
I see it clearly.

Quickly then
I make a shopping list
or rent a video.
Quickly, I look away.

Awhile back my friend Sheila came by to pay a sick visit—
I had broken a bone in my foot and for the next few weeks was
a "shut-in." Knowing of my relatively new interest in Buddhism
and in meditation, she brought me a gift, a book I began
enjoying even before I started reading it because of its elo-
quent title: *Wherever You Go There You Are.*

It's funny to travel to wonderful places when you're feel-
ing sad. You see an extraordinary painting, are surprised by
new people, partake of memorable food, are lured by a charm-
ing landscape. And for a moment, an hour, an afternoon
perhaps, you manage to lose your sad self. But of course the
book title has it right.

# Luxembourg Gardens

I sit in the shade
in the Luxembourg Gardens
a sunlit morning.
Little girls in cotton dresses,
many tourists,
fashionable Frenchwomen
perambulate.

It is quiet, soft,
someone is feeding the pigeons.
Young couples stroll,
men with packages,
distant churchbells
mark the hour.

The little café
does business
in slow motion.
The flowers hardly change
in the soft breeze.

Nothing, nothing
disturbs the peace
which eludes me.

Most of the trips I've made to Israel have been on El Al so over the years I've become accustomed to their airport drill: Why are you going to Israel? Did someone help you pack your bags? Have you been to Israel before? What will you do there? Who are you going to see? With whom will you stay?

Perhaps because my mother's been dead so many years now, I secretly enjoyed El Al's excessive questioning—it had felt to me like home. Like my mother, they seemed to care about the smallest details of my life.

My last trip to Israel though was uncharacteristically on Air France and after rather quickly getting through their security checks both coming and going, I felt by the end disappointed. Of course I know the questions are posed to sniff out terrorists or unwitting accomplices to terrorism, yet I felt when I finally landed back at JFK that no government or corporate authority cared about me or my comings or goings or my state of mind on this trip. By the time I got on line for customs, I wanted to make a full confession.

# Customs

What do I have to declare
as I reenter my country—

that I don't love the city in which I live,
that when I was abroad I was unfaithful,
coveted parks which are not mine,
that sitting in boulevard cafés felt natural,
that I've squirreled away in my suitcase
bits of wood and stone from foreign landscapes,
that I no longer feel my soul has a temporal home,
that already I am plotting my next escape.

# 10

*We All Stood Together*

Long ago now a dear friend, Rachel Adler, wrote an article for *Moment* magazine in which she analyzed some of the biblical passages that precede the giving of the Torah: men are enjoined, as part of their spiritual preparation for the encounter with the Divine, "Do not go near a woman." Rachel had essentially the same reaction to this that I had had as a young college student studying *The Ethics of the Fathers*—the pain of suddenly realizing you're not being addressed, the pain of being excluded from the tradition. But this expression of misogyny was a far more visceral and profound blow than the one that I had found in a rabbinic text—this was in the Bible itself and moreover it occurred in the midst of the holiest moment the Jewish people were to share with God. Since women were not included in this biblical passage, Rachel questioned with considerable pain whether we as women were in fact present at Sinai at all. And if we were not addressed, and we were not present, then were we even a part of the covenant with God?

I read this article in the company of friends who met monthly at that time for a Jewish feminist theology group. The group was somewhat weighted in favor of scholars, academics, rabbis. Though they made it clear that they respected me, I frequently felt inadequate. This particular winter evening, in the overheated Upper West Side apartment, I remember feeling dismayed and even a bit frightened that my feminist compatriates seemed to me quieter than usual, slower to jump in with arguments, refutations. (Later, on more careful examination of the text, it turned out that the offending words excluding women are in fact not part of God's message to Moses, rather Moses adds them for good measure when he relays God's words to the people.) But none of us saw that initially. There seemed to be no ready response.

I couldn't believe they were willing to consider this, I could hardly control my passion. "I refuse to entertain the notion that we weren't there. I won't hear of it, I won't accept it. Whatever happened, whatever pivotal, actual or mythic experience there was, it was our experience as fully as it was their experience. Maybe we have no account of it in our voice, maybe we have to recall or reconstruct or imagine what that moment was for us, but for me the premise that we were present is unshakeable, nonnegotiable."

It was already late when I left the group that evening to meet a friend with whom I was visiting overnight. It was bitterly cold, my blood was racing from the evening's discussion and my friend the insomniac, knowing how I love to dance, said, on a lark, "I've always wanted to take you to Studio 54—how about tonight?" And on a lark, I replied, "Sure." So we headed for the famous disco, the strobe lights flashing, the music splitting my ears, the rhythm vibrating from inside me, the insistent base completely overcoming me. I danced till I had no breath left to dance, soaking through the woolen turtleneck sweater, the high leather boots I had worn to ward off the frigid January air. Blissfully emptied of energy, I was ready to call it a night. Sometime between three in the morning and seven in the morning, the intellectual argument with Rachel's article, the emotional wrestling with my feminist friends and the physical release of the music and the dancing combined to wake me from my sleep on my friend's pull-out couch in the living room. I sat up and wrote about Sinai. Twice.

# We All Stood Together

*for Rachel Adler*

My brother and I were at Sinai.
He kept a journal
of what he saw,
of what he heard,
of what it all meant to him.

I wish I had such a record
of what happened to me there.

It seems like every time I want to write
I can't—
I'm always holding a baby,
one of my own,
or one for a friend,
always holding a baby,
so my hands are never free
to write things down.

And then
as time passes,
the particulars,
the hard data,
the who what when where why,
slip away from me,
and all I'm left with is
the feeling.

But feelings are just sounds
the vowel barking of a mute.

My brother is so sure of what he heard—
after all he's got a record of it—
consonant after consonant after consonant.

If we remembered it together
we could recreate holy time
sparks flying.

# Sinai

The men rushed ahead,
they always do—
in battle to defend us,
in eagerness, to get the best view,
to be there with each other
as a community.

We followed later—
some of us waited
till we were done nursing,
others waited to go together
with those who were still nursing.
Most of us were herding several children,
carrying a heavy two year old
on one hip
(it's hard to move forward quickly
with a heavy two year old on one hip).
Last came the very pregnant ones—
when you're that far along
it's your instinct to be afraid of crowds,
afraid of being jostled,
you hang back,
you feel safer being last.

Anyway, I was one of the ones
with a heavy two year old on one hip—
such a sweet body he had,
warm soft delicious flesh.
He was afraid of the noise,
he clung to me so tightly,
his fingers in my neck,
his face buried in my neck.
I showered him with little kisses,
not so much to comfort him

as out of habit
and my pleasure.

The earth shook, it vibrated,
and so did I,
my chest, my legs
all vibrating.
I sank to my knees
all the while with this little boy attached to me,
trying to merge himself back into me.

I closed my eyes
to be there more intensely,
it all washed over me—
wave upon wave upon wave . . .

And afterwards, the stillness
of a nation, a people
who had been flattened, forever imprinted,
slowly raising themselves, rising again from the earth.

How to hold onto that moment
washed clean
reborn
holy silence . . .

Not infrequently I write poems in pairs. Sometimes the poems seem wholly unrelated and I wonder why they came to me together; other times both explore the same theme from somewhat different vantage points. The preceeding two poems, written within the same few hours, attempt to express my individual and communal experience of Sinai from different perspectives, though still they share some commonality, not the least of which is a baby on the hip. I wrote them at a time when my secondborn seemed permanently attached to me, it was a triumph of will and tactical mastery to go anywhere without him. In subsequent years, building on the rabbinic midrash that we were all there at Sinai—all the Jews who ever lived and all the Jews who ever would live—I've often invited participants in writing workshops to imagine who they were at Sinai: Did you, like me, also stand with a child? Were you there as a teenager? as an old woman at the end of her days? Did you come straight from work still with your briefcase in hand? (A wonderful poem by Chava Weissler explores that image.) What did you hear? What did it feel like to you? Don't ever allow anyone to tell you you weren't there.

Both my Sinai poems are widely anthologized by now, both are included in prayerbooks. Being included in a prayerbook is unlike any other publishing experience. And then to be approached by people who say, that poem of yours, how it changed things for me, and then the story of what changed, and how . . . Of the many stories I've heard about "my Sinai poem"— *We All Stood Together* is the best known of the pair and people always refer to it that way—one of the most extraordinary came from a graduate student who informed me via e-mail, "Our family custom is to use your Sinai poem every year at our seder— the youngest girl present reads it."

A wonderful (and wacky) balance to such conversations which overwhelm and humble was provided for me by the woman whom I met at a party once. Upon hearing my name, she blinked and then blurted out, "But you're in my prayerbook—I thought you were dead!"

Many years ago, a friend with whom I'd shared years in the trenches of motherhood, came to my door late one Christmas afternoon in tears. For weeks she had worked—sewing, cleaning, baking, preparing decorations for the tree, selecting special gifts and making many by hand. Now the day had arrived. Her parents and sisters hadn't been able to come for the holiday, her husband begged off helping with the festive dinner, her kids were already tired of their presents and fighting. She was as serious a Christian as I was a Jew (in fact, she was a Mormon and I had learned over the years of our friendship that fasting and tithing were regular components of her spiritual practice.) It seemed clear to me that the obvious religious differences that separated us were less significant than the spiritual sensibilities we shared. It was no wonder that our children felt so at home in each other's homes. So I was not surprised that in this moment of religious sorrow it was my door, the only Jewish one on the block, to which she came knocking that Christmas afternoon. She wanted something both reasonable and desperate that the holiday, despite its promise, had failed to provide.

The weeklong festivals of Sukkot in the fall and Passover in the spring are, like Christmas, demanding in their preparation efforts. In the Jewish tradition, both Sukkot and Passover offer the promise of renewal, redemption—some even hold that this is when the Messiah will come. In certain communities, there is a custom that a corner of one room in the house is purposely left unpainted to signify that the world remains unredeemed, unfinished—when the Messiah comes, we will finish it. Meanwhile, we are waiting.

Often I feel, by the last day of Pesach, the last day of Sukkot—for these seven days I turned my reality upside down, and now it's over, the special time is gone. Hard to let go of the special time. Hard also to say, the special time came and went and still my mother didn't show up—I guess she *is* dead. Hard to say, I worked to make a special time but nothing has changed really.

I made Cheryl a cup of herbal tea. She talked, I listened. I shared a poem of mine with her. We both agreed it strange and funny that on that Christmas afternoon she found the poem comforting.

# I never think of myself as waiting for you

I never think of myself as waiting for you,
but then when the holiday has come and gone,
when I'm packing up the Pesach dishes
or taking down the sukkah,
I feel hopeless and alone,

inconsolable.

Then I realize
I've left a small corner
somewhere deep inside myself
unpainted,
and in that small corner,
I'm still a child,
a little girl,
waiting.

And I had hoped
without knowing it
that this *ḥag*
you'd come.

My tears fall on the Pesach dishes
and I wonder
why you've left me here
alone.

When I was a child my mother had an expression she used when she observed that I was restless, discontent, itchy. She would say, "You can't seem to find a place for yourself." On the holiday of Simchat Torah, I often feel like I can't find a place for myself.

Simchat Torah—literally, the rejoicing of the Law—celebrates the conclusion of the yearly cycle of reading the Torah: each week in synagogue, beginning with the creation of the world in the opening verses of Genesis, you read a set number of biblical chapters; at the end of the year you are up to the death of Moses, with the Israelites poised, about to enter the Promised Land. You have a wonderful party in synagogue, you dance with joy and abandon holding close the Torah scrolls, and then you begin the reading cycle all over again, back to the creation of the world.

For someone whose celebration of Jewish ritual is central, Simchat Torah ought to be the most joyous night of the year, but a number of impediments to joy have conspired over the years. Two issues especially stand out.

During the long period of time when the right of women to fully participate was in question, Simchat Torah often left us literally pinned up against the wall as the men danced with abandon, forbidding wives, mothers, sisters, and daughters from holding a Torah. I think back especially on the first or second year at Princeton, stealing a Torah from the circle of male celebrants (more accurately, Eddie and I exchanged a moments' glance and spontaneously conspired for him to pass me a Torah), leading a group of young women outside to dance with the Torah on the wet grass. While all these years later, the initial remembrance is sweet, exhilarating, if I linger awhile on the memory, what then comes up to the surface is the fear, the dread, the tension of always being engaged in battle. Especially in the '70s, if you were a feminist contemplating the observance of Simchat Torah, it was most often with several knots in your stomach: there were no safe assumptions about what the evening might hold.

But then there's the second issue, not particularly reserved for women, but a difficulty many committed Jews face—bucking the ethos of contemporary Judaism in America—still the strong social pressure to be dignified, "appropriate." Modern celebrants are constrained from entering into religious ecstasy—many don't come for this service at all, many prefer to hang back and not participate in dancing, many get around the dilemma by declaring this a "children's holiday" and pass the evening by observing their youngsters on parade. It's hard anticipating what you want to be an intense, joyful experience, knowing that all of your most powerful efforts may not be enough to incite those assembled to allow themselves to be overcome by religious ecstasy.

# I Stayed Home This Year for the Rejoicing of the Law

I stayed home this year
for the Rejoicing of the Law.
Uri had 102.4;
actually, I didn't have a sitter
anyway. I'm between sitters.

I made crepes instead.
Making crepes is soothing,
mindless—butter the pan,
pour the batter, rotate the pan
(it's all in the wrist)
cook, flip, cook, finished
butter the pan, pour the batter . . .

Cooking is different at night
alone in the kitchen
a good time to think.

I thought:
the mushrooms are beautiful,
firm, snowy white.
I'm a good cook.
I'm surprised that it bothers me
not to be there
for the Rejoicing of the Law.
I don't like it all that much
when I go.

We can't remember good melodies.
We get rough, we get silly.
We are exhibitionists.
We're embarrassed, we hang back.

What do I want? a community of ecstatics,
a community strong and fervent, hot and intense,
making love all together all at once to our Torah,
an orgy of love for our Torah . . .

I'm puzzled, that in these middle years
I find it hard to cry.

# Where are all the Jews on Simchas Torah?

The Torah waits in a corner, embarrassed.
Who will come tonight? How will they touch me?
All year I wait for this. Will my favorites come?
The girl who kisses me with her wide almond eyes,
the one who holds my smooth wood, who says
the blessings with such *kavannah*. The one who
lifts me high, unfurls me, and her face shines.

And there's a man—I shiver when he holds me
close, I feel his warmth when he carries me.
Will they all come, and more, crowding around,
a sea of humanity, ready to fast for me, to die for me?
Will they dance with me, shaking the floorboards,
will they whirl me about, hearts bursting,
making me dizzy, holding me, loving me, loving me?

Some people straggle in—
young ones proud of their ripe bodies,
eyeing each other, parents with children
flushed from being up late. They dance
and become sweaty. Someone opens the windows.

The Torah tries to make herself small,
closes her eyes and prays for a speedy deliverance.
At least in the Ark, in the darkness and silence,
there can be fantasies of how the people love her.

One of the curiosities of observing the relatively stringent dietary laws imposed for the week of Passover is that for those of us who usually straddle with ease the religious and secular worlds, during these eight days we are far more conscious than usual of where the fault lines lie.

Since I spend days prior to the start of the holiday turning my house and my kitchen upside down, I figure, in for a dime, in for a dollar—I'm not taking any chances with what I eat. So, while I can generally find on the menu at almost any restaurant something that does not violate my observance of kashrut, during this week I mostly eat only at home or in the homes of others who also observe the dietary laws.

It leaves you feeling insecure, all this attention to food, to "shall" and "shall not." It also leaves you obsessing, stocking more food in the house than you normally would, "preparing" elaborately for every brief excursion out of the house—taking along an apple, and a banana, and a plastic container of tuna fish, and a hard boiled egg, and a few carrot sticks, and some kosher-for-Passover chocolates. . .

# Broken Matzah

On the New Jersey transit train
I pulled my particularity
out of a brown paper bag:
one of four broken pieces of
buttered matzah.
Slowly, delicately,
I proceeded with my dinner.

The young man across the aisle
in his dark business suit,
pale skin, wavy black hair,
looked to me Italian
but I admit I'm not good at that.

He seemed uncomfortable,
not so much with the *chremzel*
I carefully dipped into
a little puddle of sour cream,
nor even with my public
consumption of food—
probably I was brought up
to know better, but I was brought up
so long ago I've misplaced
some of my mother's niceties—

no, I think it was the matzah
that did it, it was the matzah
that singled me out,
the unmistakable display
of my particularity:
four broken pieces of buttered matzah.

Or maybe he didn't care at all,
didn't notice,
maybe his breathing didn't
become slightly irregular,
maybe it was all
my imagination,
or my breathing
becoming slightly irregular.

How like my mother I am, after all,
who trained us in our largely
Jewish Brooklyn neighborhood
not to wear our old playclothes
outside on Sundays
so as not to offend our Christian
neighbors on their way home from church.

In those days I took her at her word;
now I wonder as the train
pulls into Penn Station
if Marie Brady who lived across the street
ever noticed us in our Sunday finery,
ever thought it curious
that we dressed up on her Sabbath,
ever questioned our carefully guarded
particularity, ever saw close up
a buttered piece of matzah.

As the wife of a rabbi, especially a rabbi who has spent most of his career working with college students, I suspect I attend more weddings than average—Eddie gets to know people when they are around the marrying age, or, even if they wait five, ten, fifteen years, they often get back in touch to ask their college rabbi to officiate. And if I know the bride or groom, I'm happy to accept the invitation to help them celebrate.

So, over the years I've been to lots of weddings—weddings in synagogues, weddings in catering halls, weddings in fields, weddings in parks, weddings on boats, weddings in libraries, weddings in arboretums . . .

Just as there's an art to paying a shiva call, there's an art to being the guest at a wedding. You're not just there to eat and network: as a wedding guest you are commanded to "help make happy the bride and the groom." I take that commandment seriously; for me it is best observed through dancing—I dance, I encourage other guests to get up and dance. I work to create a lively atmosphere, ultimately aiming for a critical mass who can sustain ecstatic dancing, lift the bride and groom on chairs, deepen the joy and add to the memories the couple will carry with them into the future.

Sometimes there are obstacles, enemies even: like the photographer hoisting a video camera, pushing aside the mother of the bride to get a better shot under the wedding canopy. And then there was the caterer . . .

# Mazel Tov!

Once
I was at a wedding
and I told the bandleader,
"When the bride and groom come in,
play something really *frailach*
because we all want to dance and lift them on chairs."

But the caterer came over, and she said,
"We're on a tight schedule here:
smorgasbord
roast beef
Viennese table
and another wedding at six.
We don't have time for dancing till after the soup."

I looked at her.
I looked at the bandleader.
My eyes narrowed, and I said,
"We'll all be dancing when the bride and groom come in
and we'll lift them on chairs.
You can play along with us, or we'll sing for ourselves."

So we did.
And he did.
And screw the caterer.

Some of us hope to find a man with whom we can share our lives, some of us are looking for the right woman. Others are content to walk a solitary path, not wanting to be intruded upon, not wanting to give the depth or intensity of what may be demanded. If we are lucky, we live in communities that allow us to be whoever it is we need to be. But many of us are not lucky.

# Esther, 28

notwife
notmother
a sitalonenik in shul

it's difficult
not to curse God
when
one by one
the little sisters
get engaged
married
pregnant

little sisters
nails in my coffin

Though I am not an Orthodox Jew, I do consider myself a traditional Jew. What does that mean? Well, for one, literally, that I value the tradition. I observe most of Jewish law with regard to Shabbat and kashrut. An engagement with Jewish texts, with the life of community, and a passion for Israel are all inextricably a part of who I am and how I have occupied my time. The cycle of my year is bound by and filled by the cycle of the Jewish year.

And yet. I do not submit to the tradition, rather I feel myself entitled to argue with it, object to it, at times to fight it. Most of all I think that has been true with regard to my status as a Jewish woman: the stories which illustrate that point can be found in abundance on many of these pages.

On balance then, my relationship to the tradition is complicated. It can be difficult to mediate such warring attractions and objections. On the one hand, I feel the powerful human need for tradition, on the other hand, how do I view a tradition when I believe it has failed to value me fully because I am a woman.

At times in my life this conflict has been personified, perhaps never more than with my mother-in-law, Rachel Feld. I can only wonder if she would have understood the feelings I articulated on the morning of her funeral as I sat to write a eulogy.

# By the light of the Shabbos candles

*for Rachel Rosansky Feld 1910–1990*

Friday afternoon
we spill out of the car,
our arms laden
with luggage and toys—
two golden children
race down the narrow hallway,
your arms their destination.

The table set,
*licht bensching,*
the men come home
from shul.
Kiddush,
then soup, chicken, fricassee,
each a celebration,
each seasoned with your love.
What my children will not
eat at home,
at your table they devour;
sated, they are put to bed.

By the light of the Shabbos candles
we sit, we talk, we read—
a new novel, an old newspaper.
The pistachio nuts dwindle
in the crystal bowl.

At your Shabbos table
I learned how sacred time
could be a home,
I came to understand
why the rabbis say
on Shabbat we have
a second soul.

None of us knows the interior landscape of someone else's marriage. I recently remarked to a friend that I thought the ones who come closest to knowing are the children who've lived in that home. This remark prompted a long conversation about her parents' marriage and my parents' marriage, after which we concluded probably the children don't know a lot either.

But not knowing doesn't stop us from speculating. Whenever some couple bites the dust, few who knew them can resist the temptation of trying to figure out what went wrong. In a wonderful movie of the 1970's, *Lovers and Other Strangers,* a straightforward, Old World father is trying to understand his son and daughter-in-law's recent separation: in a line that repeats itself over and over to ever greater comic effect, the father asks, "So what's the story, Richie?"

I suppose we want to know "what the story is" to shed some light on our own situtation: Did they break up having the same problems we do and will they now have happier futures apart? Did he become tired of the same things that irk my husband and will my husband leave me the way he left her? Did she finally decide in one particularly barren stretch of marital desert, I am actually living alone here, why not just end this and actually live alone? Weren't they once really happy, and if they were, how did they lose that and will we lose that too, are we already losing it? On and on, on and on, we look for clues, wisdom, secrets, magic, to help us navigate the difficult business of being married.

# His wife's prayer

Eddie wondered, is the point that
she's using her husband as an intercessor
to bring her prayers to God.

No I said—in these very words
she herself is addressing God, so clearly
she doesn't believe she needs her husband for that.

Rather the reverse—she is using God as an intercessor
with her husband: how can I reach him,
how can I communicate my thoughts and feelings to him.

God is right there for her—in the dough,
in the kneading, in the braiding, in the fire.
Levi Yitzhak is far away.

When you sit down to Friday night dinner, there is an order to the various acts and blessings that are part of the sacred meal. One of those sequences involves the wine and the bread—first you bless the wine, then you bless the challah. The custom is, until it's time to bless the challah, you keep it covered. Why? So that while you are blessing the wine, the challah doesn't "see" and feel embarrassed at having an inferior place on the evening's program.

Through the years, I have taken great pleasure when the challah cover is lifted, to reveal loaves of homemade bread, bread I have made with my own hands and my own time. The pride continues through to the soup, the main course, the dessert. But the pride of the homemaker is a double-edged sword—what about the weeks you come up a little short on your Superwoman routine, the weeks you are too busy, too stressed, too tired to produce a multiple course meal from scratch? And what is it that you're serving up inside that challah, what is that need to produce, that need to feed?

Just as it's important for me to bake my own challah, some weeks it's important for me not to. And not to feel diminished when I lift up the bread cover on Friday night to reveal loaves from the local bakery.

# jewish mother

Please don't
let me feed you,
let it be me
that pleases,
not the food.

It's so easy
for me to
feed you,
the dinner
makes itself,
but please,
wrestle from
me a blessing,
not rugelach,
not chocolate cake.

It's so easy
for me to
feed you—
chicken soup
or quiche—
you're on your
way? the table's
laden with
everything
you like.
It's so easy
for me to
feed you,

and shy,
withhold
myself.

In Princeton I participated in forming a Rosh Hodesh group, a monthly gathering at which a diversity of Jewish women learned to share with and care about each other. Though the tradition of Rosh Hodesh centers on the appearance of the new moon, we rarely managed to schedule our meetings on nature's cycle. Nonetheless, together we took account of our lives before Yom Kippur, together we rejoiced in the sukkah, together we studied biblical texts, together we risked interpersonal intimacy on a regular basis.

Once we spent an evening sitting together composing our own prayers. I don't remember the precise writing exercise that initiated our efforts (though I think I was the one who led that session), but I do remember an extraordinary poem written that night by Susan Reiman, one of my very favorite poets, and I remember as well one particular image that I used in what I wrote and the delight it seemed to offer Rabbi Susan Schnur. It stuck in her mind, became an affectionate point of connection for us, and years later she devoted a whole issue of *Lilith* magazine to the subject—hair.

# Still, I praise you

Afraid to call attention
to the gifts which
you have given me,
afraid that seeing what I cherish
you will take it away—

where did I learn
such deep distrust—
if I could trust you
I could praise you.

Still,
I praise you with my smile,
with my body when I dance,
I praise you with my long clean hair.

When I was in college and new to the rhythm of reading the biblical portion of the week, I was so in love with the reading and the rhythm that I remember calculating that if I lived to the age of 85, and came to shul every week, I would read each biblical portion only about 65 times. It didn't seem enough for me.

One of the things I learned as I engaged in Bible study, following the chanting of the Torah portion, participating in discussions of the reading as part of the service, was that in a text you had already read ten or twenty times, something new always jumps out at you. And so it was for me with the story of Lot and his family.

If there are ten biblical stories that stick in a child's mind, one of them is surely the story of Lot's wife (the Bible doesn't give her a name): fleeing the burning cities of Sodom and Gomorrah, she violates God's command, turns to look back toward the carnage and is transformed into a pillar of salt. Having tested my theory on a number of study groups with whom I've explored this story, I think most of us imagine her as the quintessential yenta, the very first case of rubbernecking. But then one year, one Shabbos morning sitting in synagogue, she jumped out at me. The story I had read by then maybe twenty-five times, the very same words in the very same order, revealed to me a whole new woman, a whole new story. The key to my epiphany about this narrative lies in chapter 19 of Genesis—the messengers of God who have come to warn Lot of the imminent destruction of Sodom and Gomorrah urge him to bring his entire family out of the city lest they perish in the fiery carnage; Lot then goes to speak to "his sons-in-law who married his daughters." Reading this I suddenly realized that the family of Lot is not limited to those who escape—Lot, his wife, and two daughters clearly identified earlier in the Biblical text as unmarried—suddenly I saw them, the daughters left behind. No fancy interpretation, no scholarly gloss on the text, just the simple story, waiting to be noticed.

# Lotswife

I am the no-name mother
of four no-name daughters.
The young ones, the virgins,
escaped with us.
But my first born, and
the second—the tall slim
one with the long auburn hair—
they were left behind.

He spoke to their husbands,
said we must go,
said, run away with us now.
But those two were rough
types, they scoffed and
turned their backs. My girls—
my first born and the tall
slim one with the long
auburn hair—

no one ever spoke
to them at all.

And then it was time
to go.
He said Now
Now we must go
and I ran after
him, after him as I
always had.

The heat was so intense
it licked at my heels
it burned my back
the heat was so intense.

I ran to keep up with him
at his heels I ran
as I always had
and then the tears
they flowed and burned
until finally
it wasn't a decision
to stop, to turn
it's that I couldn't see
him anymore, blinded as I was
by my tears, my burning tears.

And now it is my fate
for all time to appear
in the story, a bit player,
the scene after Abraham,
that famous scene where he
argues with God, talks with God,
enjoys the ear of God.

I come after that famous scene
blinded by my tears, my pain,
looking back, because I am
a mother and a mother
can't look away,
even when God commands it.

So I'm there in the story,
after eloquent Abraham,
without a name, without
my daughters
turning
into a tear
into a pillar of salt.

The Western Wall in the Old City in Jerusalem (in Hebrew, the Kotel) is not as some think a wall remaining from the actual Second Temple—it is only a retaining wall. Nonetheless, it is true that it is the closest relic we have of the Temple. Some people are disturbed by what they see as a dangerous tendency to turn the Kotel into a kind of idol: I agree with this view and am uncomfortable when I detect exaggerated hushed tones and false reverence.

Add to this, the problematic ownership of the site by the Israeli Orthodox establishment. The reigning rabbis utterly dictate what may and may not transpire in that place: access is limited to an "only men's" or "only women's" section, women are forbidden from conducting prayer services at the site, women may not constitute a minyan there, women may not sing prayers aloud, women may not read from a Torah scroll. Not the Judaism I have fought for. In fact, the year we lived in Jerusalem, I attended the monthly Rosh Hodesh services sponsored by Women of the Wall, a group of Israeli and international women who have been working since 1989 to gain equal access to the Kotel. Since their initial efforts to worship fully there ended several times in violence (Orthodox women and men worshippers attacked feminist worshippers), I was not unmindful the year I participated to tie up my long hair and to refrain from wearing the large dangling earrings I usually sport—I was mindful of what vulnerable parts could be grabbed, pulled, used to injure me. I was often more nervous going to the Kotel to pray on Rosh Hodesh than I was to travel throughout the West Bank to go to dialogue groups.

So, like a lot of people I know, I am somewhat ambivalent about visiting the Wall. (One of my happiest memories there is of a long morning I spent accompanied by a favorite Princeton student, tape recording the cacophony of international prayer sounds which I intended to use in the production of a play of mine. Ultimately I did not use the tapes, but my memories of the morning of taping are special. In the process, we must have witnessed twenty or more boys becoming bar mitzvah.)

A good experience for me at the Kotel usually involves going alone, losing my sense of time, absorbing fully the rays of the sun on that hot open plaza, and then making physical contact with the old stones. What happens to me there on a good morning is nonverbal.

# A visit to the Kotel

This prayer has no text,
no sound,
it is fingers warming ancient stone,
cool old stone against my hot face,
and the names of my children.

When life is humming along smoothly, when those you love are enjoying good health, when the work which provides your livelihood is secure and even fulfilling, when your biggest problem is car trouble or the babysitter cancelling, it is easy to get caught up in the little problems or annoyances of daily life: since there's nothing terrible to remind us of the proper perspective in a period when things are "OK," we sometimes forget to be joyous.

But then reality changes—the feeling that it all pretty much makes sense—gone. A new reality—you notice when you're having a good laugh because you're not laughing much these days, you don't sleep through the night anymore and don't wake up refreshed in the morning. Sometimes there are reasons why things changed—misfortunes, tragedies—sometimes maybe not.

Once when I was coming out of a dark and painful period, I said to my friend Sheila, it's as if I'm waking up. At such times, many moments every day, I feel joyous, lighthearted, aware, grateful.

The life of spirit ebbs and flows. There are times in our lives when we are open to religious experience, when we are ripe to find connection, meaning, in every stream of sunlight, in the sight of winter birds coming into formation, catching a glimpse of a now-grown daughter asleep, your eyes suddenly able to peel back the years to the child's face underneath. A hundred possibilities in nature and in human meeting. Every few days we seem to have another encounter with some new person in which we feel what is holy passing between us. Maybe those are the experiences we call Sinai.

# Sinai Again

I'm coming back to this mountain now
alone.
It's quiet,
the barren brush,
the stillness,
match my mood.

I haven't seen you in a long time God,
where've you been keeping yourself?

Me, I've had two kids,
work has its ups and downs,
I'm still married to the same man.

I don't know if you noticed,
but I stopped talking to you.
I called to you,
I called and called,
but you didn't answer,

you pushed me far away,
so far that even I
who has so little pride after all,
even I couldn't bring myself
to come crawling back—
I don't know if you noticed.

I only returned now to walk around,
kick the brush across the sand,
to walk around and think
about us.

This could be a holy place again
if you would just give me a sign—
a thrush or a hare
or a mountain goat
gracefully coming toward me.

# 11

*Brigadoon,
A Place for Dreams to Grow*

This is a story that began as a solitary story, the story of a person coming of age, growing into maturity, seeking meaning, seeking connection. The spiritual journey begins with the self: I need to articulate who I am, as precisely as I am able to see that. I need to know, in my cells, in my pores, what I am feeling. If I acknowledge that, if I honor that, I am more readily at peace with myself. But the burden of oneness, of solitude, is unbearable. Again and again we reach out for connection. Having located an intact self, I want to rub up against others, to hear their stories, to laugh, to nourish, to comfort one another, to be explorers together entering new worlds, ever deepening meaning, pleasure.

All of my life I have sought connection—in the home of my childhood; in the late night walks through Brooklyn streets with college friends on our way home from Shabbat gatherings; in the formation of *minyanim*, prayer communities where men and women sit together, are counted equally and share each other's energy in an attempt toward religious meaning; in Rosh Hodesh groups where women meet monthly to explore their relationship to the traditions they've inherited and to strive also to be active creators of new traditions; in dialogue groups where Palestinians and Jews can express honestly sources of pain, of hatred, of mistrust, and where they can lay the groundwork for new ways of living together in a space even smaller than the apartment of my childhood; in cities and towns across the former Soviet Union where women and men are finding Jewish roots again and creating a vital Jewish future; in individual friendships with women and with men where we have celebrated and struggled sometimes for decades to hear each other, to accept each other, to care for each other, to bless each other; and most of all, in the ever-changing yet solid center of my life, my adult home, where I have given love bounteously and received love abundantly and where we have made room to welcome travellers embarked on spiritual pilgrimage for the momentary refreshment offered by Shabbat, by seder, by festival celebration.

And then there's Brigadoon. Brigadoon, a place for dreams to grow, Brigadoon, which I've saved for last. *Brigadoon* was one of those wonderful Broadway musicals (later made into a movie) about a mythic Scottish village which appears from the mist once every hundred years and which has but a day for its magic to work and its stories to unfold before it once again recedes into the mist. This is one of the playful ways the women of Bnot Esh have come to refer to themselves. Bnot Esh (literally, Daughters of Fire) is a Jewish feminist community established in 1981. Consisting of 30 members, we gather once a year for a five day retreat over the Memorial Day weekend and together explore issues of spirituality, social change, and the feminist transformation of Judaism.

Why do I want to end the multifaceted story of this spiritual journey with Brigadoon? Because it is there and with those sisters that I have radically dared to explore the unknown, especially the unknown in me. It is there and with those sisters that I have again and again .been reborn, allowed the many secret selves which hide within to step into daylight. It is there and with those sisters I learned to dance without a net.

I first came to Bnot Esh in May 1984. I was 36 years old, the mother of five-year-old Lisa, and almost two-year-old Uri. Although I had already written my first play, it sat in a drawer— I knew enough to know it lacked sufficient merit to be "sent out" and in any case I had not the vaguest notion of where I might have sent it. Nonetheless, I was hard at work on a second play and had a recurring fantasy that the finished product would be so incredible that Joe Papp himself would drive down to Princeton to meet me: on a bright sunny day, he'd ring the doorbell, I'd open my front door and he would embrace me. But that was a fantasy. The reality was that I spent most of my waking hours shlepping groceries, struggling with snowsuits, lying on the floor with two kids reading Dr. Seuss. I knew in my heart of hearts I was nothing more than a mother.

What brought me to Bnot Esh? What did I know of them? I had a cordial but rather distant acquaintance with two or three group members, others were friends of friends. So it wasn't personal ties that made me say yes when they called to invite me to come on a five day retreat. It was rather my understanding of what they were about, what they did there. I sensed without knowing that these were women who, like me, cared too much about being Jewish, that the dual identity of Jew and feminist had caused them as much angst as it had me, that they were as unable or as unwilling as I to give up the fullness of one identity for the other, to compromise even for the sake of inner peace, sanity. I knew without knowing them that they were dangerous women. And I was very curious. And very hungry.

The Grail is a rambling old house in Cornwall-on-Hudson, run by a community of Catholic laywomen devoted to social activism and religious search. Opening their house for retreats to groups like Bnot Esh is a part of their work in the world. The rooms are pleasantly spartan, the food simple tasty vegetarian fare. Plenary sessions, small group meetings, and Shabbat prayers range through the common rooms of the house itself and across the fields surrounding the house.

When I arrived that first time it was already the third retreat for the group; additionally, I was unable to get there until lunchtime on Friday, though the retreat had started the evening before. I felt like an outsider, I was an outsider. There was little in the way of "orientation" for me over lunch. The morning session had been particularly intense, difficult to recapitulate for someone in the know, impossible for a stranger not yet trusted. I was left more or less to fend for myself. Twenty-three women, ranging in age from their mid-twenties to late fifties, sat in animated conversation as they ate their tabouleh and salad. They seemed to be enjoying each other immensely, laughing, arguing, gesticulating, interrupting the way comfortable friends will do. They were rabbis (by definition, pioneers), scholars, published authors, therapists, artists, social activists. They were articulate, accomplished women in the world. People paid them to speak. I thought, Merle, you're out of your league here, they're professionals, what are you—a mother. The afternoon wore on and as time for candlelighting approached, the five year old and the almost two year old back home, the children who often felt like lead weights around my neck, my time, my creativity, were suddenly distant jewels. This first Shabbos away from them stretched out before me.

Friday night rituals, Shabbos morning davening, some of it I like, some makes me uncomfortable. For moments I am drawn in, I speak now and then, I am beginning to connect names with faces, but still I feel unknown, unseen in this group. Will the whole weekend pass without my seizing the moment, some moment, to express my uniqueness, my inner turmoil, the joys and pains which define me? The tension becomes unbearable—did I need to come here and pay good money to experience my worthlessness, my invisibility? Finally, in a slot designated "free time," meant in part to be used for impromptu offerings, I ask to read some poetry I've written over the past year. I hesitate even to call it poetry, I genuinely don't know what to call it—words which have tumbled out of me, words about my children, about being a mother. Words which frighten me. Not the sentimental stuff of greeting cards, not the warm and cuddly pieties, but the dark side. Suddenly I realize that this is why I've come here, I've been looking for people who are strong enough to hear my dark words. I read, finally I look up. The women who are mothers have been crying; they look at me warmly, gratefully, I have spoken truth. The women who are not mothers look sober, stunned. So that's the truth they say.

The first lesson of building community is that everyone needs to be able to speak their truth, to come out. What do you need to enter community, to be a part of community? You need the courage to come out, to say, these are my truths, this is who I am. As one member remarked in a conversation about Bnot

Esh and community, ironically it is taking risks which creates safety, not the other way around. Often individuals will complain that this space or that doesn't feel safe to them, so they can't be authentically who they are there. But it is precisely by jumping into the void, by taking risks, that you can reestablish the group norms and find yourself at ease inside them.

To be sure, the community plays a vital role in this process—how hard or easy do we make it for you to be who you are here? Maybe we never give you a slot to read your poems, maybe once you've read them, we turn on you and say, your truth is too big for us, we are too fragile to contain your truth. That's a tragedy, for the individual and for the community. The community grows hard, rigid, ugly, shrivelled. It looks nothing at all like a flower. And the individual, the poet—we are all poets after all, writing the poem which is our life—the poet despairs, keeps the torments and the truths inside where they can be of use to no one, where they fester, causing disease and death.

Each year we come to Cornwall anew. People straggle in over the course of the day, having travelled from LA, from Philly, from Northampton, from New Mexico. We do cost sharing for transportation, also for childcare. Hugs and kisses, dragging luggage up to your room, settling in with a baby (children under one year are welcome). Most of us are present by dinnertime. But the retreat doesn't officially begin until Thursday evening when we share the welcoming ritual of a go-around. We sit in a circle in the living room and pass a watch. Each woman has three minutes to bring the community up to date on her life over the past year; your neighbor times you and when the three minutes are up, she passes the watch to you and you mark time for the next speaker.

The go-around is a particularly meaningful moment in the year for each of us, a marker in the year not unlike Yom

287

Kippur and birthdays. Where am I in the world, you ask your-self. What has this year added up to for me, what do I most want to share about that with these sisters. The obvious—I gave birth to a book this year, I'm getting married, my mother died, we've moved. But crucial facts are easy in a way. What's harder to pin down are the feelings, the deep realities of the psyche. There will be time in the next few days at breakfast, during a walk on the quiet country roads, late at night stand-ing around in the kitchen, to share details of the year that's passed, but when my turn comes in the go-around, I will hear myself articulating the essence of what my life is about.

Very early on in Bnot Esh (and for some time after that) we needed to deal with the question of structure: by tempera-ment and philosophical commitment we were non-hierarchi-cal, but none of us believed in chaos as a beneficial state. How to proceed? On every level, leadership roles are rotating—rotating and minimal.

Each year a different geographic area of the country is responsible for planning the retreat. The planning committee coordinates volunteers to be responsible for davening, to make presentations, run workshops or sit on panels to discuss the previously agreed upon agenda, the topics we have chosen to focus on for that year. Topics are wide-ranging: theology, sexu-ality, tzedukah, class, competition, body image, Israel, racism, commitment, diversity, money . . . Some topics are revisited in later years—we build on the progress in understanding we've made as a group, we see sometimes that a topic we discussed in 1992 needs to be approached anew in 2004. A simple metaphor captures the style: when you are done speaking in a plenary, you are the one to call on the next person to speak and so forth.

Clearly each of us has her strengths and comfort level in somewhat different arenas—one person makes fantastic music, another is a whiz at keeping the business meeting civil and on track, a third is at ease responding on a panel, a fourth has a gift for creating astonishing ritual. On the one hand, you don't want to lose the best of what each woman has to offer; on the other hand, one of the great values of the group is to push your boundaries and allow you to try something you don't feel so competent at. (One of my proudest Bnot Esh accomplishments was to help create the Shabbos morning davening, though it took me ten years to get up the nerve to do it and I've rarely felt such dizzying terror.)

The benefit of this approach is hopefully to stretch everyone, to avoid stagnant ways of seeing others and yourself, and to circumvent the danger of reinforcing a caste system, since some skills may be "higher status" than others. For me, the significance of rejecting hierarchy is to experience the true fluidity of the world. In a fluid universe, holiness has a better chance of breaking through.

We've learned through experience the value of going to the edge of our individual boundaries. We are always at the edge. Often it means a very high level of discomfort, anxiety, both for the person(s) presenting and for the group as a whole. You don't come to Cornwall to do the Shabbos morning service you perfected last fall in your Havurah, that Shabbos morning service that was so wonderful that everyone got high on; you come to Cornwall to do a Shabbos morning service you've never done before, one you aren't sure will work but one you've been wanting to experiment with. It's scary. Because you're offering it up to women who seem so competent to you, so accomplished, so powerful—what if it stinks, what if you fall flat on your face in front of these wonderful peers.

And sometimes it doesn't work. But the tone of the group is supportive, we try as hard as we can to enter into each

other's reality, each other's creativity, we try to be non-judg-
mental, gentle. Not only is it frightening to be the one pre-
senting, sometimes it's frightening to be the one receiving—I
can't enter into that reality, this workshop crosses my bound-
aries too profoundly. But we each work hard at trying and
often, we soar. There have been years when we felt over-
stretched and chose the next time around to take the safer
road. It doesn't work. A group which cannot tolerate tension
will sooner or later bore everyone to death. It's not enough to
come together, have a pleasant time, a lovely service, some
good laughs and go home. To give in to the yearning to be
comfortable, to give in to a failure of nerve, is a kind of death.
We come to be challenged, to be disrupted, in order to be
most fully alive, in order to grow.

Finding a sister. In August 1969 I found a sister, the first
Jewish woman I had ever known who cared so much about
being a Jewish woman, who hurt so badly over the exclusion
and second-class status of that identity in those days that she
cried over it. She cried over it.

I didn't know anyone back then besides me who cared
that much. The fact of her existence, and the companionship
of her spirit, gave me courage to push forward myself. Right
and left young Jewish women (and older ones too) were jump-
ing ship, saying, if this is the way the tradition is going to treat
me, then fuck the tradition. But my sister had a need to stick
it out, to be seen, to be heard, to be understood, to be valued.
To contribute the unique voice that is hers. And so did I.

I've watched as over the years she engaged the texts, did
battle with the tradition—see me, count me, let me sit at the
table, I have a right to be here, I have something to say. Her
journey has been different from mine—she has become a
formidable Jewish scholar, a teacher of our sacred texts, a

theologian. She happens not to be a part of the community of
Bnot Esh. I speak of her in this context because she exemplifies
for me the powerful women who are in Bnot Esh, because she
was the first for me, because knowing her taught me to be on
the lookout for such women.

Sisters. Powerful women with powerful needs. It turns
out there are a lot of us in the world. We actually can be found
all over the place. Sitting right next to you in shul, I wouldn't
be surprised if there's a powerful woman, waiting to find a
community of soulmates. Sometimes when people hear of Bnot
Esh they say, well yes, you have something very precious there,
but that's because those women are so exceptional. No. Wrong.
We have dared together, trusted together, worked together,
cried together, celebrated together, and each of us allowed the
other to see herself as powerful. We have strength as a commu-
nity in large measure because we have given each other
strength. We have been respectful of our own needs, respon-
sive to each other's needs.

But the reality of living in community is multifaceted, not
only a taste of the world to come. Sometimes—inevitably?—
living in community raises primal demons for us—do I fit in,
am I indeed a part of this group, a valued part of the group,
am I loved here, how much am I loved, would anyone care if
I disappeared? This is not the powerful voice within us speak-
ing, it is not the voice of a powerful need. A powerful need
pushes us always forward, to greater self-realization, to greater
capacities for caring, helping, sharing, achieving. No. This is
the voice of the wounded child inside of us, the child who is
insecure, needy. There's a world of difference between the
powerful need and neediness . . .

One Saturday night at Cornwall (maybe it was my third
or fourth year) the evening's program had ended and people
were scattered in the living room, hanging out in the kitchen,
sitting on the darkened porch. In small groups, in twos, in
threes. And I couldn't seem to find a conversation. Everyone
seemed absorbed, mid-conversation; it felt as if there was no

291

comfortable place for me. Though I wasn't all that tired, the hour was late, so I went upstairs and put myself to bed. I lay there in the dark, alone in a triple (my roommates for that year were still out and about), sounds of talking and laughter drifted upstairs to me and I began to cry. I felt so alone, alone only as you can feel in the midst of people who are supposed to care for you, whose caring you yearn for. And I thought, what am I doing here, I'm an outsider, why did I come back? Oh, I suppose I could go downstairs and find someone and say I'm miserable, take pity on me, but I want to be wanted, I want to be chosen.

This is not a powerful need, this is neediness, that black hole somewhere in each of us, the hole which cannot be filled, the hole which is poison for community. Some time the next day, I swallowed my pride and shared my pain. My confidante said, Merle, stop thinking about who is and isn't interested in you and how much. Think about who you'd like to have lunch with because you care about how she is, because you're interested in what she's up to and want to hear about her . . . She was right, it's an important lesson. I guess I disagree with the Wizard when he tells the Tin Man, "Remember, the heart is not judged by how much you love, but by how much you are loved by others." No. In community or one-on-one, to focus on "how much am I loved by others" is a sure way to grief. The needy hole.

It's 1988 and a major issue we have chosen to focus on this year is spirituality and class. Using one of the formats that works well for us, three or four women have volunteered (or been volunteered) to begin the plenary by presenting their thoughts on the topic. This panel will be followed by a general discussion, after which we will continue to explore the issues in small groups, giving everyone a chance to think out loud at greater length and listen to the others at greater length. Then we'll come together for a final half hour of plenary to share insights, questions.

Anytime I teach or give a talk, the preparation forces me to contemplate, research, organize my amorphous thoughts. But presenting at Cornwall provides a unique opportunity, for the audience is not only known, but intimate. And we are seekers of truth together. So I can't just speak the truth I want to speak, the truth I'm comfortable with, and let it go at that; I also feel honor bound to speak the truth which is hard to speak, the truth I find it painful to speak, even to myself.

Like any random group, we in Bnot Esh have a complex sociological mix of class at any developmental point in time. Which is to say, class status is probably more fluid than one might initially imagine: When you were a child, what did your parent(s) do for a living? What was their level of education and the expectations of that for you? for your brothers? Did the family situation change in your growing up years? suddenly a lot more money? a lot less? What effect did all of that have on your self-perception and on the self-perception of the family? What has your own education been? What have been your occupations as an adult? What status and income has resulted from those factors over the years? What is the class and economic privilege or lack thereof of your partner? of previous partners? Are you a divorced or single mother? Are you the sole provider in your household . . .

So just on an objective level, it's not unlikely that the average woman has transversed several class categories in her lifetime. And has some very strong feelings about what her class status is and about what it once was. To make my presentation I agreed to reflect on such questions and on what impact I thought class had had on my spiritual life.

I agreed to take this on because I knew that my class origins were a central factor in my identity formation and I'd never before that point in time forced myself to examine the impact of that. This was a part of myself I rarely shared with others, or looked at squarely for myself, or experienced in the context of others who struggle with their own stories. I could not have predicted the pain or the power of the work of preparation, or presentation. It represented a profound "coming out" for me. Many of the insights about class and spiritual life that are expressed in these pages had their origin in the presentation I delivered for that Bnot Esh session. I came to understand that we don't come out just once in a group, but over and over—pain, vulnerability, new growth in self-understanding. And there isn't always a happy ending, a neat resolution. Sometimes we do come in conflict with each other in community and it doesn't lead to a greater mutual understanding and closeness, sometimes it leads to a real breach which defies reconciliation. But community, when it's working well, provides the challenge, the context, and the support to explore dangerous questions. And the work goes on all our lives.

I remember it happening my first year at Cornwall, before we lit Shabbos candles. One of the people leading Friday night davening asked us to gather in groups of four and to take turns giving each other an "aura brush" before Shabbat. In each small group, three of us encircled a fourth and, using our hands, made sweeping motions in the air, moving carefully from head to toe of the woman whose "aura" was being brushed. (She had her eyes closed, and felt only the motion of air.) Once you reached her feet and had fully swept away the cares and troubles of her week, you reversed the process and moved the air around her upward with your hands, this time whispering softly her name, beckoning her refreshed Shabbos soul. Each of us in turn had our aura brushed, stood with eyes closed as our Shabbos soul was called forth. It was playful, sweet, loving. A gift.

Another year, Shabbos morning. The California women were leading davening. We were instructed not to come down to the davening space as usual, but rather each to wait in her own room, the door open. The five prayer leaders started at the top of the rambling old retreat house, singing. Debbie Friedman's *Lechi Lach* was new; again and again we heard the verses as floor by floor, room by room, each woman in turn was invited to prayer. "To a place that I will show you . . . *lechi lach* . . . to a place you do not know . . . " If you were amenable, they anointed you with perfume, they gave you flowers . . . "on your journey I will bless you . . . And you shall be a blessing . . . you shall be a blessing . . . *lechi lach* . . . " Finally, all together in the davening room, sumptuous baskets of dates and figs, cashews and almonds, flowers, singing . . . my heart is bursting. California davening, encircled by love, I am ready to pray . . .

It's Saturday night and our faithful popcorn maker is hard at work in the kitchen. Hot topics for discussion come and go, forms for doing *misheberahs*—special healing prayers— come and go, even group members come and go, everything changes, but Saturday night popcorn is a constant. Even in a community this intense, especially in a community this in- tense, you need to be ordinary together, whimsical, you need to share all the pieces of the secular culture you grew up with and still live with day to day. It's Saturday night and three of us wind up singing show tunes together. "I got the horse right here, his name is Paul Revere" . . . Sometimes others listen, sometimes others join in, it doesn't really matter to us if there's an interested audience or not: somehow this is one of our powerful needs. Girls growing up in a certain era in Brooklyn, in Queens, they know the lyrics to every song Rodgers and Hammerstein ever wrote, they are surer of Lerner and Loewe than the order of the morning service, and at least once a year there's deep pleasure in "If ever I would leave you" . . . big finish, girls—"you'll neever waaalk alonne . . ." Saturday night, popcorn, *Guys and Dolls*. These too are rituals.

Living in community offers us the opportunity to be most authentically ourselves. Telling the stories which are uniquely and intimately our own, then finding in the eyes of the listeners understanding, affection, respect, is the unparalleled gift which community has to offer. And what is it that we need to create such communities? Courage, it always comes back to courage.

# 12

*Readers' and Writers' Guide*

As I remark in the preface to this revised edition, I have observed that encountering the poetry and prose in this book has given readers across the country and around the world the opportunity to explore, articulate and better understand truths about their own lives and stories. I have relished the many opportunities I've had to personally use poems or prose selections from the book as a teaching resource—sometimes offered as a springboard for discussions in which participants felt free to share more deeply and soulfully than common social etiquette permits, sometimes offered as prompts to writing, inspiring individuals to journal about their own joys, challenges, tragedies and the small daily events in their lives that might otherwise go unnoticed. It is now with great delight that I share the benefits of those teaching encounters with you, the reader, putting in your hands the means by which you can similarly further enrich your own reading experience, unlocking the mysteries and surprises of your own spiritual journey.

For some of you that will mean using the materials in the book as a framework or spark for discussion, for others it may mean journaling in conversation with the themes highlighted in this chapter. I hope that the seven sessions I have developed for this Guide, sessions which bear the fruit of so many cherished evenings, mornings, and afternoons spent with women and men in living rooms, in synagogues, in college classrooms, at retreat centers, will now offer you possibilities for opening and for new spiritual vitality.

## Using *A Spiritual Life* for group study: format and techniques

Let me begin by saying that whether you are using this resource for your ongoing book group, as the curriculum for an adult ed course, for some special gathering of your synagogue community, for an interesting evening with friends and family, for an academic course you're teaching, or in an informal learning environment, this guide is meant to be suggestive. My recommendation is that you select from among the sessions—and within each session, from among the questions—that which calls to you, that which seems applicable or relevant for your particular purposes. And by all means, feel free to adapt, improvise!

If your group is small (eight or under) then it's probably best to have your discussion altogether. But if the group is larger than that, and certainly if it is much larger than that, I have found that a greatly enriched experience is provided when for some of the session time participants study in pairs (when used for traditional Jewish text study this is called a *chevrusa*).

Here's how it works: the group begins all together, then breaks into pairs to explore and share the texts one-on-one, then all the pairs come back together for further plenary conversation. In this way, everyone gets lots of time to talk and express ideas, gregarious participants don't wind up dominating while shy folks remain quiet and underinvolved, and people paired together generally experience one another in a much deepened way. You will find that there is an intimacy created through this format that can be profound since it's only natural that we feel "safer" and are more willing to share one-on-one than in a large plenary where personal remarks may perhaps feel too risky or inappropriate.

Also consider as an alternative or an addition to *chevrusa* study, structuring your session so that participants can talk together in small groups of threes or fours for some part of the total time and then reconstitute as a whole group. Mixing and matching in this way offers an added layer for thoughtful creativity in preparing a satisfying conversation.

These techniques of *chevrusa* study or small group conversations may be implemented for perhaps forty-five minutes to an hour out of a one-and-one-half-hour session. Begin with everyone all together and briefly introduce an overview of *A Spiritual Life*, the specific theme(s) under discussion, and provide some simple prep about process. Then break into subgroups or pairs, asking people to take turns reading the poems or prose pieces under discussion and then suggesting that they focus on the questions provided. For the next part of the program, gather all the pairs or small groups together again to further develop ideas and to share. You may choose to close with asking participants to reflect a bit on the process they've just been engaged in: What was this experience like—with this text? with each other? Do you have some new awareness of yourself? of your study partner(s)? What is special about this way of talking together? Where might you/we want to go next in this process—where has this study taken us as a group/class/community?

I have found that *chevrusa* study and small group configurations actually work best when people are asked to partner with someone they don't know, don't know well, or don't often have the chance to interact with one-on-one. [Note: If you are using more than one session from this chapter with the same constituency, mix up the configurations of pairs or small groups so people can have experiences with a larger circle over time.] These formats offer a wonderful strategy for stimulating the formation of mutually respectful groups when people have gathered initially as strangers. Further, again and again I've witnessed a flourishing of warmth and cohesiveness result from such sessions in preexisting communities, with people who have sat at a polite distance perhaps for years suddenly seeing each other as if for the first time. The payoffs often reach far beyond the session itself in the ongoing life of a group or community.

## The benefits of text study

All the sessions I've developed in this chapter invite participants to closely attend to a few short texts—as you can see, each grouping of poems and/or prose pieces focuses on a particular theme. Such an approach comes in equal parts from my experience with the model of traditional Jewish text study and my experience studying literature in graduate school. In both venues I have always found that the richest and most intellectually and personally satisfying discussion arises from just such a concentrated engagement with specific texts.

Further, out of my long experience as a teacher of texts, let me recommend that at the outset of discussing a particular poem or prose selection, you begin by briefly recapping together the simple straightforward level of "what's happening," the journalistic who-what-when-where-why. That way everyone in the conversation is starting on the same page.

You will want to allow sufficient time for participants to be able to talk in depth. If people will be working in pairs, I'd recommend allowing for about ten to fifteen minutes of discussion per poem—the larger the number of people in the group studying together, the more time each part needs for the conversation to open, deepen, breathe. In any case, it's always good to check in and ask people if they are ready to move on or if they need a bit more time. In most sessions I've selected three or four poems because I think they facilitate a full conversation about each theme, but you may decide to trim the possibilities further.

## What if you're reading this book solo: try journaling

If you've been reading this book solo, I would first of all encourage you to empower yourself to create a group to share the book with! (Approaching a significant *yahrzeit* for my mother, I once invited a few friends to gather for an evening's conversation in which we each talked about our mothers—I created a series of questions for us to consider to help describe who our mothers were or had been, their dreams, their hopes, their life struggles, their life stories, some of the complexities of our relationships with them. Though it sprang from my particular need, the evening was unquestionably evocative and rich for everyone present.)

But what if you've just finished reading *A Spiritual Life*, want to continue in relationship to the ideas, themes, questions, issues, but feel for whatever reason that group sharing is not the way you'd like to go at this moment in your life? Buy yourself one of those old-fashioned hardcover black-and-white marbled composition notebooks at a twenty-first century version of the corner five-and-dime, and spend some time sitting with the questions in this chapter, responding to them and moving beyond them as you write. **Note that in each of the seven sessions, some of the questions provided for reading groups are specially marked in bold font—these questions do double duty, intended both for those engaged in group discussion and also intended for solo readers as suggested writing prompts.** I invite you to reread the selected poems or prose pieces and then to be in conversation with them, with me, and with yourself as you journal.

The questions are an invitation to take half an hour here and there and give yourself the gift of quiet time that emerges in a special way when we write. I've worked to create these writing prompts to help you identify and focus on introspective questions that can be fruitful to explore. Sit quietly, arrange not to be disturbed for a while (maybe go out to a coffee shop or the local library for refuge) and listen for your own voice as you have listened for mine while you were reading. Let the questions open doors deep within you and feel yourself supported and accompanied by the same truthful spirit that inspired this book as you move through those open doors into the chambers of your own spiritual life.

For some time now I've perceived a need for a book about writing as a spiritual practice, a field I have pioneered, but for the meanwhile that book is stuck in a queue behind compelling teaching commitments and putting the finishing touches on a new collection of poetry. Please accept this revised edition of *A Spiritual Life* and the suggestions for journaling that follow here as a promissory note for a forthcoming book devoted to writing as a spiritual practice.

In conclusion, I believe this uncommon Guide offers you a wide range of meaningful opportunities and I hope you will enjoy using it. Please feel free to contact me at merlefeld@yahoo.com to share your thoughts about the Guide and about this revised edition as well.

# 1 ∞ What is a spiritual life: Encountering spirit in everyday moments

(Remember to begin by reading the poem aloud together and then briefly recapping what's going on in the poem.)

### *Supermarket Prayer,* pp. 207–208

Is there a regular time of day that you go to the supermarket? (Do you go? If not, what's your equivalent of a public place you regularly need to frequent?) Do you think about how you look before you go? How do you feel about running into people there? As the shopper in this poem, what is it that I "see"? Can you sin against someone just by virtue of having seen them? What would constitute kindness here? What would constitute *tikkun olam* (an act of repair or healing)? **Think of some specific people in your own life, in your community, who are in need of help: How might you be an agent of healing, how might you be of help?**

### *Mazel Tov!,* p. 261

Have you ever been present at such a *frailach* (lively) wedding? As a wedding guest here, what is it that I do? How do you feel about what I do? **Remember a particular time when you were present at a potentially powerful spiritual moment: What sort of moment was it—baby naming? engagement party? funeral? Shabbat dinner? retirement party? Fourth of July picnic? . . . Did you do something to help the moment realize its potential? If so, what was it you did? If not, why not, what held you back?**

### *The Nap,* pp. 63–64

How do I as a young mother in this poem seem to feel about my daily routine? Would you imagine I view some/all/none of my day as being spiritually charged? What is the significance of the last line of the poem? **What are the details of your daily** routine? Where within your typical daily routine do you see openings for spiritual experience?

*My father in his chair,* p. 121

What do we know about the father from this poem? Why is he looking through old photographs? What is the process he seems to be engaged in? Describe his favorite picture. What might be its significance? **Do you know/have you known anyone engaged in this process? What does he or she need from you? How might you share with them? learn from them? be of help to them?**

*Suggested last part for everyone together:*

**What does "spiritual" mean for you? What does this tapestry of poems suggest to you about enriching your own spiritual life? In the private and public spheres, how might you help more moments to flower spiritually?**

# 2 ∞ The life of the soul: I belong to myself

Prose Piece: "A memory that repeats itself..." pp. 5–6

This is one of my earliest memories—why might it have left such a strong impression? What are all the ways this day at home is different for me as a child? What seems to be the lesson of "the special book"? of being shut out of synagogue attendance for lack of money?

What is the significance of this mother saying, "Please don't disturb me"? What does it mean in this story, "I belong to myself"?

What is striking to you about my family's Yom Kippur observance? **[For those who are Jews from birth]: How is my childhood experience of Yom Kippur like/unlike a Yom Kippur experience you may have had as a child? [For all]: What powerful moment(s) can you recall from your own childhood, at home, in synagogue, or elsewhere, watching the adult(s) "talk to God"?/not "talk to God"?**

**When did your mother say, "I belong to myself"? Was it hard for her? easy? regular? rare? Tell that story about your mother.**

**When do you say, "I belong to myself"? Has it been a struggle for you to say that, and if so, why? What has the evolving process of that been like for you? Tell about what it's like for you to do that.**

# 3 ∞ The life of the family

### *Yizkor*, pp. 134–135

How would you characterize the nuanced relationship I have as a daughter with my mother in this poem? **Have you lost a close loved one, and if so, is it hard for you "to remember something real" about them? What do you remember?** How does humor work in this poem? What do you imagine it means for me to say in this context, "I'm all grown up now/completely grown up now"? **At what point in your life did you feel yourself become an adult? What constitutes "adulthood" for you?** How do I as a daughter seem like/unlike my mother here? **How are you like/unlike your same sex parent?**

### *The First Fight*, pp. 115–116

This poem tells one story in the relationship between a daughter and father: What do you find significant about this particular moment between them, and what does "the fight" seem to convey about the larger context of their relationship? What in the poem resonates for you as familiar and what seems unusual? Why does this daughter keep repeating "it was my job to make conversation"—what gender dynamics might be in play? **Do you recall "the first fight" you had with your father? Tell the story, reflect on its meaning. How old were you? Was it hard for you to fight with your father?** What's the significance of the poem's last stanza? What do you think the last line means? **Do you wish the "space" between you and your father was smaller? greater? How might you achieve the degree of space you'd like?**

### *His wife's prayer*, p. 267

There are two different couples in this poem: Pearl and her husband, Levi Yitzhak of Berditchev, a late-eighteenth-century rabbi in the Ukraine, and a contemporary American woman and her rabbi husband. What does the poem's epigraph tell us about how Pearl and Levi Yitzhak communicate with one another? What relationship does Pearl have to God? to her husband? Do we get any sense from the poem of how the modern husband and wife communicate? What are the connections in the poem? the disconnections? **[If you are partnered]: What challenges do you find in communicating with your partner? what strengths? How do you and your partner find connections?**

Prose Piece: "The haze of those early newborn days . . . ," p. 62

**[For those who are parents]: How does this description of first-time parenting evoke your own concerns, experiences, memories as a new parent? Remember and share the details of a particular story of yours. What opportunities did you have or make to talk about your fears and insecurities as a new parent? What might be the advantages of doing so openly? Who helped you and how? How might you offer support to new parents in your extended family or in your community?**

*Yom Kippur Break,* pp. 80–81

Why do you think this conversation takes place on Yom Kippur? What is the mother in the poem afraid of? **Do you as a parent share such fears?** How is the parent/child relationship that's described in this poem similar or different from the parent/child relationship in *The First Fight?* **How do you think we as parents can care for ourselves emotionally as our children struggle to grow up and separate?**

*Further suggestions for group conversation and/or journaling:*

Choose some other poems or prose pieces from chapter 4 (Report from the Trenches) that also speak powerfully to you— plan a second meeting around those selected texts with a few focus questions to spark conversation. **Or continue your journaling on those themes.**

# 4 ∞ Faith and doubt: How we talk with God

*The first time we made Shabbos together, p. 88*

Who is present in the poem? What are some of the character-
istics of "first times"? What is my relationship to God in this
poem—why am I thanking God, what do I seem to feel God
has done for me? What is the poignancy of juxtaposing "You
have been so good to me" with "Finally, for the first time in my
life/you gave me something I wanted . . ."? How can those two
statements be reconciled with one another? What is unspoken
in the poem—a "gift" from God that goes unmentioned?
**Remember, and share the story of, a special moment in your
own life when you were full of rejoicing, praising God: What
were the circumstances, the details, of that moment? [or] Re-
member, and share, a moment when you felt especially blessed.**

*Croup, pp. 75–76*

This poem seems to exist in two parts: How and why do you
think that is so? As the frightened mother of a sick child, what
is my relationship to God here? What do the last two stanzas
make you feel—can you untangle all the emotions in them?
**Do you ever feel/have you ever felt this way toward God?
When? If you feel ready, begin to tell that story.**

*Sinai Again, pp. 279–280*

Of the three poems in this section, this one seems most di-
rectly centered on the relationship to God: What problem do
I, as a woman in midlife, seem to be having with God? What
do I want? What is the sign I seem to be looking for? (Are
there "signs" in the earlier poems? What are they?) **What has
been/what is your experience with prayer? What do you want
from a prayer experience? Do you feel you're addressing God
when you pray? If not, what are you doing? What outcome are
you hoping for from a prayer experience?**

# 5 ∽ Community: a place for dreams to grow

> Prose Piece: "All of my life I have sought connection . . . refreshment offered by Shabbat, by seder, by festival celebration." p. 283

What are the varieties of "community" referenced here? Do they share any common elements? What are all the varieties of community that are operative for you? **Note that I include in this catalogue the home I created and have welcomed others into—does it seem to you that a home can function as locus for community? Does your home sometimes function that way?** Also unexpected perhaps is the inclusion of Israeli-Palestinian dialogue groups—why do you think I include them? **What are some of your experiences with community—as a child? as a teen? as an adult? Which groups or communities have suited you best? What was it about the individuals involved or the collective that succeeded in meeting your needs for connection? What have been challenges or obstacles to your finding community?**

> Prose Piece: "What brought me to Bnot Esh? . . . And I was very curious. And very hungry." p. 285

Why might I as a newcomer to the group refer to these women (especially perhaps in the early 1980s) as "dangerous"? Why do I seem to see myself as, like them, "dangerous" and what do you think is meant by this characterization? **How do you intuit what sorts of people might be potentially compatible, nourishing, for you? What does "community" mean for you; what do you want or need from community? What characteristics or signals do you look for when searching for a community?** This group, Bnot Esh, had existed for two years before I joined it—how is it different to enter an already existing group v. participate in the group's formation? **How would you go about/how have you gone about finding or creating a community to sustain you, to fill your needs for connection? [If you're reading this book solo, and journaling, how does it feel for you to be solitary while considering these questions?]**

Prose Piece: The first lesson of building community is that everyone needs to be able to speak their truth . . . how hard or easy do we make it to be who you are here . . . the poet despairs, keeps the torments and truths inside, where they can be of use to no one . . ." pp. 286–287

Why might I have experienced reading my poetry in this context as being courageous, a "coming out"? Why do you think it might have been important to me to risk that? Would you agree that an important element of community is to be able to speak your truth? **What feels difficult, what feels like "coming out" for you in a group? Can you remember times when you have taken risks in a community? What resulted? Have you**  **ever regretted doing so? How do you feel when you decline to take a risk in such a situation?**

Prose Piece: "One Saturday night at Cornwall . . . This is not a powerful need . . . The needy hole." pp. 291–292

Is it shocking to read about such vulnerability in an adult? **Can you recall times in a group when you have felt as fragile, insecure? As a child? As an adult? How did you handle your**  **vulnerability and what do you feel about it now, looking back? What did you learn from the experience?** What do you think of the advice the confidante offers? **How might this have been**  **a learning experience** and why do you think I tell this story as part of a chapter exploring community? **How might you diagnose and address where the problem lies when you feel troubled in the context of community (with you? with the group? some combination?), and what are the dangers, challenges, and opportunities of such moments?**

# 6 ∞ Tikkun Olam: The road to getting involved

Prose Piece: "When I was growing up in Brooklyn, my mother didn't read the *New York Times* . . . I felt at home in their homes." pp. 148–149

What messages did I seem to get growing up about moral responsibility and political involvement, and how did gender and class play a role in that? **What were the messages you got growing up about social/political involvement—from family? friends? at school? in your [Jewish] community? Did you have models of people engaged in activism? men? women?**

**When did you first become politically/socially aware? What internal inhibitions or familial/cultural conditioning did you— or do you—have to overcome in order to empower yourself as an agent for change?**

*Friday in Jerusalem,* p. 145

What is the "sadness" in this poem and what seems to be its effect on me? Does the "disconnect" I seem to experience between feeling and action strike a chord for you? **What *particular* social/political situations—locally, nationally, internationally—weigh most heavily on you? Have you been able to take action, find opportunities to engage and mobilize to work toward bringing change? What inner and outer challenges or difficulties impede you?**

*The Visit,* p. 151

What kinds of movement occur in this poem? What are the varieties of irony? Are there purposes served by this "visiting"? How is the feeling of this poem different from *Friday in Jerusalem?* How do I as a nascent activist seem different in the two poems? Does this activism seem productive? meaningful? **What actions to try to bring about change have you undertaken that perhaps met with mixed success? How do you evaluate the efficacy of your activism? What situations have you learned** and grown from? How might you more effectively use your time, energy, and talents to help find solutions for the many problems we face today?

Prose Piece: "Women in Black," pp. 146–148

In what ways do I appear to feel challenged by my participation in Women in Black and why might I view that participation as epitomizing my transformation? How does the increasing activism of my year in Jerusalem, and the crucial first-time mentoring by Veronika, seem to lead naturally to the commitments and involvements detailed in the following chapter, *Repairing the World: The Work of Tikkun Olam?* (Interesting to note that *Friday in Jerusalem* describes me in a solitary state, whereas all my subsequent activism involves working with others.)

*Suggested last part for everyone together:*

Have you found ways of embodying your social commitments in the world? If not, how might you begin to do so? Have you been able to find mentors and/or partners for change making? Are you currently committed to particular activities or causes? What is difficult for you about this work? When working for change, what meaning, reward, or growth has this work afforded you? How has the work of making change changed you?

313

# 7 ∽ The Power of Shabbat

The poems in this section are especially full of people—young lovers, old friends, family members across generations, partners in activism, impressionable undergraduates—people actually present and people imaginatively present. As you consider each poem, be especially aware of who is present, what is transpiring, and how the mood is or isn't changed by the different personae. (Be sure to check the glossary for Hebrew and Yiddish words found in the poetry.)

*The first time we made Shabbos together,* p. 88

Interesting that this is the first poem in the chapter titled *Passion*—why might it have been placed there, rather than in the chapter on Jewish tradition and holidays? (It seems fitting reading this poem to remember that Shir ha Shirim, Song of Songs, has traditionally been considered both a human love poem, and also a love poem between God and Israel. In this poem it seems almost impossible to separate how the beloved is human and how the beloved is Shabbat.)

Where do you find humor in the poem? How is the stage set in the first half of the poem? Why is "And then you made kiddush" on a line of its own? Why do I weep? What does it mean to have the soul of Ein Gedi? What is unspoken in the poem? What role does Shabbat play here?

**Remember a Shabbos moment, perhaps a Friday night dinner, perhaps a moment at another time of the day, that you experienced as especially beautiful—what made it so, what made it special, unique?**

*On the other side of the world,* p. 102

Veronika figures prominently in the *Israel* chapter of this book as a dear friend and powerful mentor in peace activism—what might be the significance of dedicating this poem to her? Why might I be thinking of Veronika as I move from the work and busy-ness of the week to a state of rest and peace? What is the "reaching out" that seems so important in the poem? What do you think it means, "in all my best prayers"?

**How do you begin Shabbat? Do you light Shabbos candles, or participate in candlelighting? If so, what spiritual function does candlelighting serve for you? Who is present for you (as Veronika is present in this poem) during candlelighting? Tell a story about how this soulmate has nourished you. Where do you "go" (what happens within you) in private ritual moments like candlelighting? What is the relationship between that "side trip" and the recitation of the formulaic prayer?**

**Do you have a context (with family? friends? community?) for making Shabbos? Can you have a solitary Shabbos? Interesting—like *The first time we made Shabbos together*, this poem is also located in the chapter *Passion*: Does that suggest a heightened love energy present on Shabbat? Is that congruent with your experience of Shabbat?**

*By the light of the Shabbos candles*, p. 265

We know from the prose which precedes this poem that it was written and delivered as a eulogy for my mother-in-law. In this multigenerational family, there are different cultural and religious traditions present—what are indications of that in the poem? in the book as a whole (e.g., see the following prose selection)? How do these generations relate to each other? What is passed down from the older generation to the next? Is there indication of mutuality in the sharing of particular Shabbat family customs and rituals? How might that present difficulties?

**What are the different generations in your extended family like? Do they come from different faiths? different streams of Judaism? Have they found ways to appreciate, respect, one another's differences? What are the challenges inherent in that process? How might the Jewish community in all its varied splendor better learn to practice pluralism?**

Prose Piece: "But Sukkot comes only once a year, Pass-over comes only once a year, Shabbat is a weekly oppor-tunity for creation . . ." pp. 44–47

What feelings are evoked for you reading about this Shabbos table? Does it surprise you that I put in many hours a week "making Shabbos," going to such pains to make the evening possible? Why do you think I say that over the course of a lifetime, making Shabbos is "perhaps the single activity which has most consistently and profoundly defined meaning for me"?

I call my Friday night dinner table "a spiritual art form"—how is my preparation for Shabbat an expression of my creativity? I refer to homemade challah as "bread on its way to a holy moment"—what other attention is paid to food, aesthetics, creating a scene, a special mood? Does it seem to you neces-sary or important to go to so much trouble?

This is clearly a very important religious ritual taking place, not in a synagogue but in a home—what do you make of that? Presumably the many guests appreciate the gift of sharing such an evening, but how do you imagine they themselves enrich the Shabbat celebration through their presence and participa-tion? How is the "art" of hosting different from the "art" of being a good guest?

Each of the preceding selections in this *Power of Shabbat* sec-tion represents an image of Shabbat—how are the various portrayals different from this one? What if anything do you think they have in common? Which of the four scenes seem closer to your own circumstances at this time of life?

### Suggested last part for everyone together:

**Do any of the modes of celebrating Shabbat described here appeal to you? seem desirable or possible for you to attempt given your own current reality? How might you enhance your Shabbat observance? How might you borrow or adapt some of these rituals, aesthetics, practices to fit your own circum-**

stances—for example, lighting Friday night candles and enjoying some tasty take-out? inviting over a friend to study/eat/sing/talk with? exploring the possibility of your local synagogue sponsoring Shabbat home hospitality? organizing a pot-luck dinner yourself with a group of other overly busy but spiritually-seeking friends/family members?

Good Shabbos!

# Glossary

bikur cholim—(Hebrew) the religious injunction of visiting the sick

chremzel—a fried cheese patty made with matzah meal and beaten egg; an Eastern European delicacy made in some homes on Passover

daven—(Yiddish) to pray

Echa—the Book of Lamentations, chanted to a special melody on Tisha B'Av

Ein Gedi—(Hebrew) a spring and oasis in the Judean desert, referred to since biblical times

frailach—(Yiddish) lively, festive

ḥag—(Hebrew) holiday

kavannah—(Hebrew) religious intentionality

kiddush—(Hebrew) blessing over the wine

Kislev—(Hebrew) month in the Hebrew calendar that falls during November/December

licht bensching—(Yiddish) in traditional homes the women light candles before sunset on Friday evening to welcome the Sabbath make Shabbos—to do the shopping, cooking, and cleaning necessary to prepare a home for the observance of the Sabbath and then to celebrate the day of rest

minyan—(Hebrew) a quorum of ten adult Jews, required for full public prayer service

mitzvah—(Hebrew) strictly speaking, that which was/is commanded by God; in common parlance it means "a good deed."

Pesach—(Hebrew) the festival of Passover that commemorates the exodus from Egypt; special dietary requirements are in effect for this holiday and in traditional homes separate dishes and cookware are used

shuk—a Middle Eastern market, in this case the large fruit and vegetable market Mahane Yehuda located in downtown Jerusalem

shul—(Yiddish) synagogue

Simchas Torah—(Yiddish) literally The Rejoicing of the Law (though never referred to so literally); the holiday on which the reading of the Torah scroll is completed and then begun anew; a particularly joyous holiday with dancing integrated into the worship service

sit shiva—to observe the Jewish laws of mourning; paying a shiva call is to visit someone in mourning

slicha—(Hebrew) sorry

sukkah—(Hebrew) a harvest booth in which it is traditional to eat meals, built to be used for the seven day festival of Sukkoth

Talmud—the body of Jewish tradition comprising the Mishna and Gemara, generally published in oversized leather-bound volumes

Tisha B'Av—the ninth day of the Hebrew month of Av when Jews observe a day of mourning to commemorate the destruction of the First and Second Temples in Jerusalem and the subsequent dispersion of the Jews

yahrzeit candle—a 24-hour candle kindled to commemorate the anniversary of the death of a close relative

yizkor—(Hebrew) to remember; prayer service of remembrance

# Index of Poems

# Literary Sources

"Healing after a miscarriage" first appeared in *Response*, Spring 1985

"Meditation on Menstruation" appears in *Four Centuries of Jewish Women's Spirituality*, eds. Ellen M. Umansky and Dianne Ashton, Beacon Press 1992

"Birthing Blessings" appeared in *Response*, Spring 1985

"The Nap" appeared in *Response*, Spring 1985

"Report from the trenches" appeared in *Response*, Spring 1985

"My Friends Baked Cake and We Ordered Lox and Whitefish from the Deli" appears in *Sarah's Daughters Sing*, ed. Henny Wenkart, Ktav 1990

"Croup" first appeared in *Response*, Spring 1985

"The first time we made Shabbos together" appears in *Sarah's Daughters Sing* Ktav 1990

"Jerusalem, I write your name" appears in *Reading Ruth*, eds. Judith A. Kates and Gail Twersky Reimer, Ballantine Books 1994

"On the other side of the world" appears in *Reading Ruth* Ballantine Books 1994

"Happy Birthday Merle" appears in *Lifecycles* Vol. I, ed. Rabbi Debra Orenstein, Jewish Lights Publishing 1994

"And then there's my father" appears in *Lifecycles* Vol. I Jewish Lights Publishing 1994

"Though I Stared Earnestly at my Fingernail" appears in *Lifecycles* Vol. I Jewish Lights Publishing 1994

"The Warmth of the Sun" appears in *Reading Ruth* Ballantine Books 1994

"Yizkor" appeared in *Tikkun* September/October 1993

"The Visit" appeared in *Challenge* (an Israeli magazine) Vol. II, Number 4 July–August 1991

"Bikur Cholim" appeared in *Challenge* Vol. II, Number 4 July–August 1991

"Tisha B'Av" appeared in *Tikkun* July/August 1991

"A beautiful shining face" is adapted from *Across the Jordan* published in *Making a Scene,* ed. Sarah Blacher Cohen, Syracuse University Press 1997

"Supermarket Prayer" appears in *Worlds of Jewish Prayer,* eds. Shohama Harris-Wiener and Jonathan Omer-Man, Jason Aronson 1993

"Moving ahead moving on moving along moving" appears in *Lifecycles* Vol. II, eds. Rabbi Debra Orenstein and Rabbi Jane Rachel Litman, Jewish Lights Publishing 1997

"We All Stood Together" first appeared in *Kol Haneshamah, Sabbath Eve Prayerbook* The Reconstructionist Press 1989

"Sinai" first appeared in *The Journal of Feminist Studies in Religion* Fall 1985

"I never think of myself as waiting for you" first appeared in *Lilith* 1988

"Mazel Tov!" appears in *Sarah's Daughters Sing* Ktav 1990

"By the light of the Shabbos candles" appears in *Reading Ruth* Ballantine Books 1994

"Lotswife" appeared in *Tikkun* September/October 1994

"Sinai Again" appears in *Worlds of Jewish Prayer* Jason Aronson 1993

Material in chapter 1 describing the founding of Havurat Shalom has been adapted from an essay of mine, "Egalitarianism and the Havurah Movement," which appears in *Daughters of the King,* eds. Susan Grossman and Rivka Haut, JPS 1992.

Chapter 10, "Brigadoon, A Place for Dreams to Grow," appeared in an earlier version in the journal *The Reconstructionist* Vol. 60, Number 1, Spring 1995.

Material in chapter 7 has been adapted from "At the Crossroads" in *Reading Ruth* Ballantine Books 1994.

# About the Author

Merle Feld is a widely published poet, award-winning playwright, peace activist, and educator who has pioneered teaching writing as a spiritual practice. Her prose and poetry, including her signature poem about women and men at Sinai, "We All Stood Together," can be found in numerous anthologies and prayerbooks. Feld's highly acclaimed memoir, *A Spiritual Life*, has been translated into Russian and enjoys a wide audience across the former Soviet Union; a Hebrew translation is forthcoming. Her theatre credits include *Across the Jordan*, published by Syracuse University Press in the anthology *Making a Scene*, and *The Gates are Closing*, performed by hundreds of congregations worldwide.

A popular teacher internationally, Feld has facilitated Israeli-Palestinian dialogue on the West Bank and at Seeds of Peace and has also worked with grassroots community organizers in the former Soviet Union. She serves as Founding Director of the Rabbinic Writing Institute, established in 2005, guiding rabbis-in-training across the denominations to develop and explore their own spiritual lives and to more effectively serve as spiritual leaders.